FINANCIAL REFORMS IN EASTERN EUROPE

Of all the East European post-communist states, Poland has followed the most radical approach to transforming its centralized economy into a market economy. The 'big-bang' approach it adopted had never before been attempted on such a large scale, and it was a dramatic departure from the more gradualist processes favoured by countries such as Hungary and the Czech Republic.

In this study, Gupta and Lensink present a model that simulates the effects of financial reforms in transitional economies, which they then apply to Poland for a variety of policy simulations. In a sequential manner, the authors develop models for households, commercial banks and firms, expanding their enquiry into the government sector, the central banking sector, the external sector and finally the supply side. These sub-sector models explicitly incorporate institutional features specific to the Polish economy. The estimated model is used to simulate the effects of a wide array of financial policies introduced in Poland, and these results are then used to assess the effectiveness of the policies analysed.

This is a timely and authoritative study which sheds new light on how a country's overall economic system responds when it pursues a 'big-bang' approach to marketization.

Kanhaya L. Gupta is Professor of Economics at the University of Alberta, Canada. **Robert Lensink** is Associate Professor in Economics at the University of Groningen, The Netherlands.

ROUTLEDGE STUDIES OF SOCIETIES IN TRANSITION

FINANCIAL REFORMS IN EASTERN EUROPE

A policy model for Poland

Kanhaya L. Gupta and Robert Lensink

London and New York

First published 1998
by Routledge
11 New Fetter Lane, London EC4P 4EE

Simultaneously published in the USA and Canada
by Routledge
29 West 35th Street, New York, NY 10001

Typeset in Times by RefineCatch Limited, Bungay, Suffolk
Printed and bound in Great Britain by
TJ International Ltd, Padstow, Cornwall

British Library Cataloguing in Publication Data
A catalogue record for this book is available from the British Library

Library of Congress Cataloging in Publication Data
Gupta, Kanhaya L. (Kanhaya Lal), 1935–
Financial reforms in Eastern Europe: a policy model for Poland /
Kanhaya L. Gupta and Robert Lensink.
p.   cm. – (Routledge studies of societies in transition)
Includes bibliographical references and index.
(hardbound : alk. paper)
1. Finance – Poland – Mathematical models.   I. Lensink, Robert.
II. Title.   III. Series.
HG186.P7G86   1998
332′.09438 – dc21   97–48957
CIP

ISBN 0–415–16668–3

FOR JONATHAN, KARUNA AND ANS

CONTENTS

FIGURES

TABLES

ACKNOWLEDGEMENTS

Kanhaya Gupta would like to thank the Research Institute Systems, Organizations and Management (SOM) of the University of Groningen and the Netherlands Foundation for Scientific Research (NWO) for funding his visit to the University of Groningen to work on this book. He would also like to thank the Faculty of Economics for its facilities and its hospitality. In particular, he would like to thank Robert Lensink for his invitation to visit, for his friendship and for making his stay a real pleasure. Thanks are also due to the participants of the conference on "Coping with Financial Reform in Emerging Market Economies: Analytical Tools, Policy Implications and Case Studies of Estonia and Poland", held in Poznan, 20–21 January 1996, for comments on an early version of Chapter 6 of this book. The funding of Robert Lensink's visit to the Poznan conference was supported by the European Commission's Phare/ACE programme 1994 under contract number 94–0685–R. Special thanks are due to Charlene Hill for, once again, helping with the typing of the manuscript. Finally, we would like to thank the referees of the publisher for constructive comments.

1

INTRODUCTION

Ever since the demise of the former Soviet Union, the economies of Central and East European countries have drawn considerable attention. This is because of their attempts to move away from the highly centralized systems to a free market regime. While many other countries have also been trying to move in that direction, these economies constitute a special case because of their centralized structures. In a way they offer almost a controlled experiment going from one extreme to another. And no country exemplifies such an attempt more than Poland. This is because of its adoption of the so called "big bang" approach when Solidarity first came to power in 1989. While it would be interesting to analyze not only all of the countries of the former Soviet empire and also all policies designed to achieve the desired market orientation in these countries, that would be a task beyond any single volume. Our aim is more modest and restrictive. What we hope to achieve in this short monograph is to confine ourselves to three countries: namely, the Czech Republic, Hungary and Poland as a background and then concentrate on Poland. However, while the exercise is specifically carried out with reference to Poland, our hope is that the model proposed and the estimates and the data series constructed are prototypes of the transition economies and thus have broad applications in this region.

Even for Poland, our interest is narrowly defined. We are entirely concerned with the implications of financial reforms and their effects on the Polish economy. This particular aspect of economic policies, both in Poland and other transition economies, has attracted considerable attention, as will become evident in the chapters to follow. In this introduction, we briefly explain what we want to do and provide the outlines of the chapters to follow.

As pointed out above, Poland is a fascinating case study because of the fundamental break from the past in 1989. The break was so radical that one could not really appeal to its past to examine its current economic policies. This poses both analytical and practical challenges. Analytically, while the temptation to model the Polish economy along the lines of standard neoclassical lines is enormous, that would be a mistake because of its special institutional features and its very rapidly changing environment, not only economic, but also institutional in the widest sense of the word. The data problems are formidable. Most of the new series that are relevant to our study start in 1990 or 1991, so that on an annual basis there is virtually nothing one can do. Even using quarterly data we would not have enough observations for any meaningful estimates. Therefore, the only option is to use monthly data. Here, while monthly data on some of the financial variables are generally available, such is not the case on virtually any of the real variables. The preparation of the appropriate data series was thus a major task. Therefore, we consider the data Appendix to be a major contribution of this study. We also provide a relatively comprehensive bibliography in the area.

It is not a ground-breaking observation to say that for a proper understanding of the role of financial reforms in the Polish – or for that matter in any – economy we should construct some sort of a general equilibrium model, which can at least clearly identify some of the mechanisms through which financial reforms of various types affect different aspects of the economy concerned. It is also widely accepted by now that single equation reduced form approaches are not very enlightening because they reveal virtually nothing about the mechanisms via which any given variable affects the dependent variable concerned. But, as we shall see later on, precisely such models have been widely used in the analysis of various types of policies in the transition economies. This is not the approach used in this study. Instead, we follow a general equilibrium approach. However, the term "general equilibrium" is used more in the nature of macro models rather than the detailed CGE type models.

The basic approach of this study then is as follows. We distinguish five economic agents: households, commercial banks, firms, the central bank and the central government. We then use the balance sheet of each of these agents and model its components. The modelling of the components is consistent with the requirements imposed by the balance sheet. Since the assets and the liabilities in each balance sheet also appear in one or more of the other balance sheets, the cross balance sheet requirements are also imposed. This allows us to design an internally consistent model, which allows for interactions between the behaviour of the five agents identified above. Once the behaviour of these five agents has been modelled, we move on to the supply side as well as the external side of the economy. The model introduces nominal wage and price rigidity. A rationale for these features is offered. In the specification of the models for the three private agents, namely, the households, the commercial banks and the firms, we follow a uniform approach. That approach consists of the Tobin type portfolio selection approach. It has not only the virtue of providing us with a unified framework, but also provides a very rich menu of mechanisms through which financial variables may affect the real and the nominal variables. However, within this framework special consideration is given to features specific to the

Polish economy. In the assets and the liabilities modelled for the three agents identified above, we have carefully followed the ones identified in the official Polish data rather than impose any prior categorization. This has been very instructive because the composition of the various portfolios in Poland has undergone radical changes over the six years studied and our disaggregation allows us to capture some of these changes. Because of data constraints and the need to keep the model both understandable and useful, we have confined ourselves to modelling the effects of those aspects of financial policies which are being used most often by the central bank and the commercial banks in Poland, although the model we propose is flexible enough to allow for further extensions.

It is important to point out that we are not interested in building a model for its own sake, but rather so that it can be estimated and then used for policy analysis. In short, the parameterization is not based on guestimates or borrowed values, but on actual estimates of the model using Polish data. In estimation and specification of the complete model, we follow a sequential approach. That is, we first specify and estimate models for each chapter separately, then we bring all of the components together and test for consistency as defined above. The robustness of both the sectoral as well as the entire model is checked by *ex post* forecasts of the dependent variables. For illustrative purposes, we also report policy simulations for each sector. This may be construed as a partial equilibrium approach. These experiments have some merit in themselves in that they are derived, not from some reduced forms or single equation models, but from the portfolio approach, so that they provide some check on the suitability of the approach to the policy issues being examined. A detailed outline of the chapters now follows.

Chapter 2 sets the stage with a brief review of the major economic changes in the Czech Republic, Hungary and Poland since 1990, as well as summaries of some of the work done to explain those changes. This chapter tries to highlight the important changes that need explanation.

Chapter 3 models the behaviour of the Polish commercial banks. Following the data given in the various issues of the bulletin of the central bank (henceforth called NBP), it first identifies the main assets and liabilities. Their portfolio then consists of the following assets: loans to firms; loans to households; net foreign assets; excess reserves; and government securities, separately in the form of T-bills and treasury bonds. The liabilities consist of borrowing from the NBP.

The model in this chapter tries to explain the observed changes in the portfolio composition. This is done by specifying a Tobin like portfolio model. Using the budget constraint for the commercial bank, the adding-up and the symmetry restrictions are derived. These restrictions are used in the estimation procedure. An important feature of the estimates reported is that the interest rates, wherever relevant, are the real rates and net of taxes. Furthermore, an important feature of the commercial banks in Poland is the very high default rates of loans to firms. These high rates imply a lower loan rate. We pay special attention to the modelling of this feature. Effectively, this means specifying loan rates as being net of the default rate. The "fit" of the estimated model is judged by comparing the within-sample dynamic forecasts with the actual values. Finally, the chapter reports some simulations regarding the effects of changes in the various rates of return.

Chapter 4 models the household sector. This chapter tries to build on the model presented in Gupta and Lensink (1996). There are two distinctive features of this model. The first is that it treats the decision to consume and the portfolio decision as being simultaneously determined rather than sequential, which is the common practice. As Gupta and Lensink (1996) explain, this simultaneity has far-reaching implications for examining the effects of financial policies. The second feature is the incorporation of the financial balance sheet of the Polish households into the model, just as we do in the case of the commercial banks. A very special feature of the household portfolio in Poland is the role that foreign currency-denominated deposits, both demand and time, play. To ignore this feature would greatly distort any analysis of the Polish economy as far as modelling the effects of financial policies is concerned. The main assets for this sector then are: currency; zloty demand and time deposits; foreign currency demand and time deposits; and net foreign assets. On the liabilities side, there is borrowing from the commercial banks.

Since the portfolio behaviour and consumption behaviour of this sector are modelled as being simultaneous, particular attention is paid to defining the income of the households. This, as can be seen from the next chapter on firms, has implications for their behaviour. The basic model in this chapter is the same as in Chapter 3 for the commercial banks. In the specification of the equations for the various assets and consumption, particular attention is paid to the role of credit constraints on the households and to the role of taxes and inflation. Quite apart from the fact that it is reasonable to assume that households react to after-tax real rates of return and not to gross nominal rates, this kind of modelling allows financial policies to affect real behaviour in interesting ways. The issue of adding-up and symmetry restrictions is carefully addressed.

The estimated model is once again used for two purposes. First, to examine whether it fits the data adequately. This is done, once again, by performing within-sample dynamic forecasts. Second, a number of illustrative partial equilibrium policy simulations are carried out to check the effects of changes in the various rates of return on the portfolio composition of the households.

Chapter 5 is devoted to the behaviour of the Polish firms. The basic approach here is the same as in Chapters 3 and 4. Therefore, we proceed by first identifying the components of their balance sheet and then by using a similar portfolio framework, specifying a model explaining the behaviour of various assets and liabilities. As explained in Chapter 2, one of the more popular but contentious issues in Poland, when it comes to firms, is the role of credit and its cost. We pay particular attention to this issue, by specifying the role of commercial bank loans and their cost in the various assets and liability equations, including the investment equation. This allows for a much more comprehensive and integrated role for credit. Not only does it allow for the direct effects of credit constraints on investment, but it also allows for indirect effects via changes in the entire portfolio composition of the firms. These changes may well be important if firms hold significant other assets: say, for example, foreign assets or government bonds. The basic approach of the rest of the chapter is the same as in Chapters 3 and 4 as far as estimation, within-sample forecasts and partial policy simulations are concerned.

Chapter 6 builds a complete version of the model. For this model we bring together the three sub-models developed in Chapters 3, 4 and 5 and supplement them with the behaviour of the other agents identified above. More specifically, we deal first with the behaviour of the Polish central bank (NBP). Our basic approach in this case also remains the same. That is, we start with its balance sheet and identify the main assets and liabilities. As a preliminary, we examine recent changes in the balance sheet. We then look at some of the factors underlying the observed changes. Next, we look at the behaviour of the central government. In this case, we proceed by examining the behaviour of the government with respect to the financing of its expenditures. Since the Polish government, like most others, systematically runs budget deficits, it must find means of financing it. The major issues that have characterized the debate in Poland on this issue have revolved around the role of the central bank and that of the commercial banks in financing budget deficits. At another level, it has revolved around financing by short-term T-bills or long-term bonds, regardless of who buys them. We then specify the budget constraint of the government. Since the assets and liabilities in this case appear elsewhere in the four other balance sheets, we specify appropriate consistency conditions. Assuming constant prices (fixed price model) and ignoring the foreign sector, this gives us a self-contained model that can be solved for all the endogenous variables.

But we do not assume away either the external sector or the supply side. The external sector is modelled quite simply. The exchange rate in Poland is based on a "crawling peg" system and we model its behaviour relatively simply. We do the same thing for the net trade balance. Modelling supply side was quite a bit problematic, because of the difficulties in constructing data on capital stock and the rates of capital utilization. So we use a Cobb-Douglas production function with constant returns to scale and derive the values of its coefficients from observed factor shares. We assume that the goods market is continuously cleared by prices, thus assuming perfect price flexibility. However, we impose some nominal wage rigidity. Therefore, we model the demand for labour by the usual marginal productivity condition and the behaviour of nominal wages via a simple Phillips type curve. Labour supply is assumed to be exogenous.

The entire model is checked for consistency in the sense that the various balance sheets are consistent with each other. In order to see whether the estimated model fits the data adequately, we report a few within-sample dynamic forecasts.

Chapter 7 addresses the issue of policy applications of the model. Since our main purpose in this study is to examine the implications of various financial policies, we confine ourselves to the effects of those instruments which are used most frequently by the central bank and the commercial banks. The central bank uses the reference rate or the discount rate and the various required reserve ratios as the most common instruments of monetary policy. It is well known that high required reserve ratios drain liquidity from the system and can adversely affect the supply of loanable funds to the household and the firms which can be quite detrimental to consumption, savings and investment, particularly if both households and firms are credit-constrained as would seem to be the case in Poland. Since the NBP imposes differential required ratios on the four types of deposits, two zloty and two types denominated in foreign currency, we examine how changes in various required ratios affect the major macro variables, like, inflation, GDP, balance of payments and unemployment rate. The rationale for the particular ratios used is not clear, so our simulations might shed some light on the relative ratios imposed.

The second set of policy simulations relate to the effect of changes in the reference rate. Here we proceed in two alternate ways. First, we assume that the other rates do not change immediately in response to the central bank rate changes. There is some evidence to support this point. The alternative assumption is that they do, but with a lag. The simulations in this case are meant to shed light on the effectiveness of discount rate policy. Of course, a comparison of the simulations with the required reserve ratio changes could shed light on the relative effectiveness of the two instruments.

Turning to the effects of policy changes induced by the commercial banks, we consider two sets of rates: those on banking loans to the firms and the rate on zloty time deposits as a representative of the rates on four types of deposits. As for the effects of changes in the deposit rates, there are various possibilities here. For example, do identical changes in the four rates have different effects? If so, how different are they and in what sense? Would it be better for the economy if the banks attracted zloty time deposits rather than the other three types of deposits? How significant is the role of foreign currency-denominated deposits in the transmission mechanism of changes in the domestic deposit rates?

Loan rates can affect both the supply of credit and its cost to firms and the households. As mentioned above, the issue of high loan default rates is very important in Poland. What would happen to changes in the loan rates under alternative assumptions about the default rates? What would be the effect of ignoring the issue of default risk? Are cost effects more important than credit supply effects of a given change in the loan rate?

In the policy simulations suggested above, there are certain features of the model which are exploited. For example, it was pointed out above that in the case of the households we use an integrated model of portfolio selection and consumption. We examine the sensitivity of the simulation results to this assumption by assuming the more traditional approach in which such interdependence does not exist. We could reasonably argue that as Polish consumers become more sophisticated and the financial markets mature, the interdependence between the two decisions can only increase. So, our simulations are meant to shed some light on this phenomenon.

Chapter 8 offers a brief summary of the major findings and the lessons that can be derived from our modelling exercise.

2

A STATISTICAL OVERVIEW

There is substantial literature which describes the economic events in the three countries which are the subject of this chapter. Therefore, no attempt is made to be exhaustive. Instead, we highlight some of the major economic changes that have taken place in these countries over the last five years. Since the financial sector is dealt with in the next chapter, it will not be considered here.

Our story essentially starts in 1990, when economic reforms really took over in these economies. An overview of the major changes is given in Tables 2.1, 2.2 and 2.3. The first thing we notice from these tables is the well-known dramatic decline in the growth of the gross domestic product in 1991 and 1992. Much has been written on the causes of this precipitous contraction. We'll have more to say on this later in the chapter. But we can also see a gradual recovery in all three economies since 1992. Thus, in 1995 the growth rate had climbed to 4.3 per cent in the Czech Republic, to 1.5 per cent in Hungary and to 7 per cent in Poland. Despite the differences in the rate of recovery in the three countries, the patterns are very similar and this raises the interesting question of what were the common factors characterizing all three economies? We do not pursue this question in this study, although we hope that the estimated model for Poland and the policy simulations based on it will shed some light on the underlying factors.

Structural and other changes

Since the dominance of the public sector had been one of the major defining features of the economies now in transition, it is useful to look at what has been happening to its role over the past five years. While the data are not available for the most recent years, none the less we can see from the data in Table 2.4 for the shares of the private sector in GDP and employment that its role has been shrinking in all three countries. Thus the share of the public sector in GDP had shrunk to about 40 per cent in the Czech Republic in 1993; to less than 50 per cent in Hungary and Poland by the end of 1993. A similar situation existed in terms of the share of employment, though to a

Table 2.1 Selected data: Czech Republic * (% change)

	1989	1990	1991	1992	1993	1994	1995 est.
GDP at constant prices	1.4	-.4	-14.2	-6.4	-.9	2.6	4.3
Private consumption at constant prices	na	na	na	20.4	2.9	5.3	9.2
Gross fixed investment at constant prices	na	na	na	8.9	-7.7	4.4	na
Industrial production	.8	-3.5	-22.3	-7.9	-5.3	2.3	na
Consumer prices (annual average)	2.3	10.8	56.7	11.1	20.8	10.0	10.0
Broad money	3.5	.5	26.8	17.3	20.5	21.5	na
Share of agriculture in GDP	6.3	8.4	6.0	5.7	6.2	5.5	na
Share of industry in GDP	na	na	na	45.0	39.8	39.3	na
Interest rate (3-month interbank deposit rate)	na	na	na	13.8	13.2	9.1	na
General government balance % of GDP	-2.8	.1	-2.0	-3.3	1.4	1.0	0

*Transition Report, 1995, EBRD

Table 2.2 Selected data: Hungary * (% change)

	1989	1990	1991	1992	1993	1994	1995 est.
GDP at constant prices	.7	-3.5	-11.9	-3.0	-.9	2	3
Private consumption at constant prices	-.3	-.8	-5.8	-.5	1.4	1.2	na
Public consumption at constant prices	.2	2.6	-2.7	3.9	30.5	-22	na
Gross fixed investment at constant prices	8.8	-7.8	-10.0	-2.7	1.73	11–12	na
Industrial production	-1.0	-9.6	-18.2	-9.8	4.0	9.5	6
Consumer prices (annual average)	17.0	28.9	35.0	23.0	22.5	18.8	29
Broad money	13.8	28.7	28.5	26.8	15.5	13.4	na
Share of agriculture in GDP (%)	9.7	9.6	8.6	7.3	6.4	6.6	na
Share of industry in GDP (%)	30.1	28.8	25.5	26.4	25.2	25.9	na
Interbank interest rate (14–30 days maturity year end)	na	na	35.4	15.4	21.8	31.3	na
Central government balance % of GDP	-.8	.8	-4.4	-6.9	-6.6	-7.7	-5.0

*Transition Report, 1995, EBRD

Table 2.3 Selected data: Poland* (% change)

	1989	1990	1991	1992	1993	1994	1995[1]
GDP at constant prices	.2	−11.6	−7.5	2.6	3.8	5.0	7.0
Consumption at constant prices	6.1	−11.7	7.2	3.5	5.1	1.2	5.7
Gross fixed investment at constant prices	−2.1	−10.6	−3.1	2.3	2.9	7.0	na
Industrial production	−1.4	−26.1	−11.9	3.9	5.6	13.0	9.4
Consumer prices (annual average)	251.1	585.8	70.3	43.0	35.3	32.2	23
Broad money	236.0	121.9	47.4	57.5	36.0	38.2	21.6
Private sector share of GDP (%)	28.6	31.4	45.3	48.2	53.5	56.0	na
Agricultural sector share of GDP (%)	7.8	8.4	9.3	8.3	7.1	na	na
Industrial sector share of GDP (%)	49.5	43.6	39.2	39.6	37.8	na	na
Interest rate (rediscount rate, end of period)	136.0	48.0	36.0	32.0	29.0	28.0	na
General government balance % of GDP	−7.4	3.1	−6.5	−6.7	−2.9	−2.5	−3.1

* Transition Report, 1995, EBRD
[1] Plan Eco

Table 2.4 Private sector share in GDP and employment*

	1989	1990	1991	1992	1993	1994	early 1995
In GDP							
Czech Republic	11.2	12.3	17.3	27.7	45.1	56.3	56.5 (guess 70% in mid-1995)
Hungary	14.9	–	33.0	44.0	52.4	–	
Poland	28.6	31.4	45.3	48.2	53.5	56.0	
In employment							
Czech Republic	1.3	6.9	18.8	31.1	47.1	–	
Hungary	–	–	–	–	–	–	
Poland	45.7	45.8	51.1	57.0	57.6	59.8	

*Transition Report, 1995, EBRD

slightly lesser extent. This trend toward increasing share of the private sector, of course, is the result of deliberate policies and we shall have more to say on this later in the chapter.

Another aspect of structural change is in terms of the share of industry in GDP. Here we do not have very recent data for any of the three countries, but from what we do have, the share was about 68 per cent in the Czech Republic in 1991, 25 per cent in Hungary in 1993 and about 40 per cent in Poland in 1992. In terms of the data for 1989 it would appear that the share had gone down to some extent. This deindustrialization may seem surprising at first, but when we consider the fact that state sector was shrinking but the private sector was not expanding at the compensatory rate, this outcome is not surprising.

It is also useful to look at the behaviour of inflation. In the Czech Republic – with the exception of 1991 when it reached a high of 57 per cent, which might have had something to do with the extreme contraction in the GDP – it has not shown signs of such resurgence, although it still remains high by North American standards. In Hungary, inflation has remained in the neighbourhood of about 20 per cent since 1990, while in Poland it has steadily declined from a high of 585 per cent in 1990 to 23 per cent in 1995. On the whole though, inflation rates have been higher during this period in Poland than in the other two countries. Whether this differential reflects their differential experiences in terms of their growth rates or other factors is a moot point.

What stands out from this very brief survey is that after the precipitous decline in 1991 and 1992, recovery seemed to have taken root in all of the three countries, though at different rates. This takes us to a brief examination of some of the possible factors underlining the early contraction and the subsequent recovery.

Table 2.5 Gross domestic investment as percentage of GDP (current prices)*

	1985	1989	1990	1991	1992	1993	1994
Czech Republic	28	27	29	30	24	17	20
Hungary	26	27	25	21	15	20	21
Poland	28	39	26	20	15	15	19

*Transition Report, 1995, EBRD

Table 2.6 Gross fixed investment as percentage of GDP (current prices)*

	1985	1989	1990	1991	1992	1993	1994
Czech Republic	26	26	26	23	25	23	27
Hungary	23	22	19	19	20	18	20
Poland	21	16	21	20	17	16	16

*Transition Report, 1995, EBRD

Early contraction: why?

As we saw in the last section, there was a sharp decline in output immediately following the initiation of reforms in all three countries. It is now widely conceded that even if we allow for measurement problems which might have exaggerated the decline reported earlier, the decline is none the less steep, which calls for an explanation. As one might expect, there is no consensus on the causes. But, broadly speaking, we can distinguish two main explanations: those which centre around the "structural change" hypothesis and those which emphasize the traditional demand and supply factors, although even here there is no unanimity on the relative importance of demand and supply factors.

Just to give a brief flavour of the controversy, perhaps the best known approach of the "structural change" school is exemplified by Blanchard (1997). He develops a two-sector model with the sectors being the state and the private sectors. The basic idea is that the state sector shrinks in response to policies towards a market economy, but the private sector is not able to expand enough to absorb this shrinkage, thus leading to net decline in output and employment. Of course, there can be a variety of factors which may hinder the expansion of the private sector, including shortage of working capital, experience and so on.

This reallocational hypothesis was tested by Borensztein *et al.* (1993) for Bulgaria, the Czech and Slovak Republics and Romania. They did not find any support for the hypothesis. Instead they reported that almost all of the variations in output could be accounted for by aggregate factors.

There is no consensus on the relative importance of demand and supply shocks either. Thus, Borensztein *et al.* (1993) reported that supply shocks were the dominant factors in the case of Bulgaria and the Czech and the Slovak Republics, but that the results were inconclusive for Romania. Berg and Blanchard (1994), on the other hand, reported that for Poland the decline was largely explained by the demand factors, and that the supply factors like the credit availability were of little significance. But Calvo and Coricelli (1992) contradicted Berg and Blanchard and argued that the initial decline in output was the result of supply constraints, which were in turn caused by a shortage of working capital.

What is clear from this brief review is that most likely a variety of factors were responsible for the earlier decline and that what we need is a general equilibrium type of a framework which would allow for the role of various factors. The studies reported above as well as the others not summarized, use partial equilibrium approaches. While our study is not aimed at explaining the phenomenon of the early contraction of output, none the less we believe that the model we propose will be useful to analyze that question in a more suitable framework.

The banking sector

The broad aspects of the banking sector in the three countries are summarized in Tables 2.7, 2.8 and 2.9. Table 2.7 highlights the size of the banking or the monetary sector in these economies. It is measured by the ratio of broad money to GDP. Two things stand out from the data. First, that the banking sector is not that important yet. And second, that even in that respect, there

Table 2.7 Indicators of financial sector developments *

	1986–89	1990	1991	1992	1993
Broad Money (% of GDP)					
Czech Republic/CSFR	68.9	67.9	71.4	83.3	78.2
Hungary	49.1	48.0	57.8	61.5	37.3
Poland	47.6	32.6	31.7	36.0	34.1
Currency to deposit ratio					
Czech Republic/CSFR	14.0	15.5	14.5	13.4	9.01
Hungary	31.0	26.4	23.8	23.0	24.3
Poland	22.5	24.8	27.4	23.4	23.2
Household foreign currency holdings % of financial assets					
Czech Republic/CSFR	.3	3.5	8.0	13.6	13.6
Hungary	1.5	15.0	20.9	18.5	22.6
Poland	40.4	57.8	47.2	44.7	48.6

* Dittus (1994)

Table 2.8 Bad loans as percentage of total loans *

Country	% and year
Czech Republic	19 (1992)
Hungary	28 (1992)
Poland	20–30 (1995)

*Dittus (1994) for Czech Republic and Hungary. For Poland, see *The Financial System in Poland*, Bank Gdanski S.A., 1995.

Table 2.9 Net enterprise borrowing from domestic banks as percentage of GDP

Country	1990	1991	1992	1993
Czech Republic	2.6	6.4	2.9	5.5
Hungary	1.1	1.6	−2.5	1.6
Poland	7.3	8.0	1.1	3.3

* Dittus (1994).

are significant inter country differences, with Poland having a ratio less than half of that of the Czech Republic. A further indicator of the as yet under-developed nature of their monetary sector is the role still played by currency as a financial asset in the household's portfolio and as a medium of exchange. This is shown by the ratio of currency to deposits. While the Czech Republic again stands out among the three, the ratio of 24 in the other two is more akin to that of a developing country than a developed country. Finally, the foreign currency holdings as a proportion of financial assets reflects on the so called "dollarization" of these economies. The figure of 48 per cent for Poland is particularly noteworthy and will have a bearing on the modelling of the Polish economy as will be seen in the following chapters.

Another distinctive feature of the banking sector in the transition econ-omies is the high proportion of "non-performing" loans. For the three countries, some information is given in Table 2.8. The importance of these loans for the commercial bank portfolio behaviour as well as for the role of financial liberalization will be explained and modelled in the chapters to follow. What is noteworthy here is the high proportion of these loans.

Finally, the importance of the banking sector can be looked at in terms of its role as provider of credit to enterprises. This information is given in Table 2.9. This table shows that net lending, as a percentage of the GDP, varied widely between the three countries, with the ratio being as low as 1.6 for Hungary and 5.5 for the Czech Republic. But the intertemporal behaviour of the ratio for the three countries was remarkably similar. Two points are par-ticularly noteworthy. First, the increase in the ratio for all three from 1990 to

Table 2.10 Progress in transition (by mid-1995)*

	Private sector share of GDP% in mid-1995	Enterprises		Markets and Trade			Macro Control	Financial Institutions	
		Large scale privatization	Enterprise restructuring	Price liberalization	Trade and foreign exchange system	Competition policy		Banking reform and interest rate liberalization	Securities markets and non-bank financial institutions
Czech Republic	70	4	3	3	4*	3	4	3	3
Hungary	60	4	3	3	4*	3	3	3	3
Poland	60	3	3	3	4*	3	3	3	3

*Transition Report, 1995.

Notes: In each case, the ratings are 1, 2, 3, 4 and 4* with 4* indicating standards and performance typical of advanced industrial economies.

Large scale privatization: 3: more than 25% of large scale state owned enterprise assets privatized. 4: more than 50% of state owned enterprise assets privatized.

Enterprise restructuring: 3: significant and sustained actions to harden budget constraints and to promote corporate governance effectively.

Price liberalization: 3: substantial progress on price liberalization including for energy prices. 4: comprehensive price liberalization.

Trade and foreign exchange system: 4*: standards and performance norms of advanced industrial economies.

Competition policy: 3: some enforcement actions to reduce abuse of market power and to promote a competitive environment.

Macroeconomic control is measured by the rate of inflation.

1: inflation above 100% in 1995;

2; inflation between 50 and 100%;

3: inflation between 10 and 50%;

4: inflation under 10%.

3: substantial progress in establishment of bank solvency and of a framework for prudential supervision and regulation; full interest rate liberalization with little preferential access to cheap refinancing; significant lending to private enterprises and significant presence of private banks, securities markets etc.

3: substantial issuance of securities by private enterprises: establishment of independent share registries, secure clearance and settlement procedures, and some protection of minority shareholders; emergence of non-bank financial institutions and associated regulatory framework.

1991. When we recall the fact that output declined during the same period, this increase in net lending raises some interesting questions. Second, the increase in the ratio from 1992 to 1993, which is also remarkable in terms of the magnitude. One has to wonder about the role of credit availability in the subsequent recovery. Our estimates and the simulations reported later on should be able to shed some light on this question.

The march towards a free market economy: progress so far

Much has happened since the initiation of the reforms in 1990. No single reference provides a more detailed account of the changes so far than the Transition Report 1995 published by the European Bank for Reconstruction and Development. We summarize the relevant information in Table 2.10.

Since a detailed explanation of the information given in Table 2.10 is provided in the Transition Report, we highlight only some of the features. We first note that all three countries have made substantial progress in all aspects of the move towards a market-oriented economy, but at the same time more remains to be done. More specifically, in terms of the privatization of large enterprises, only Poland has some way to go yet, but in terms of the restructuring of the enterprises, all three have some distance to go. Regarding price liberalization, all three countries still have some work left to be done. In terms of interest rate deregulation, much has been achieved, but more needs to be done. Finally, in terms of the success of their stabilization efforts, as measured here by the rate of inflation, the Czech Republic has done remarkably well, while the others would seem to be moving towards a goal of a reasonable rate of inflation, but have much work left. Of course, this last feature reflects the control of the growth rate of money supply as well as the budget deficits.

This statistical review has been admittedly brief, but it is deliberately so. The intention is not to provide the history of reforms in these countries but to simply highlight features which we hope to capture in our modelling efforts reported in the chapters to follow.

3

COMMERCIAL BANKS[1]

This chapter looks at the first building block of the model for the Polish economy, which is the main objective of the book. We begin by considering the portfolio behaviour of the commercial banks. In particular, we are concerned with analyzing the main changes that have taken place in the composition of the portfolio and the main factors which may have accounted for the observed changes. For this purpose we proceed by describing the main changes in the composition of their portfolios and then look at the behaviour of the various rates of return. This is followed by a simple Tobin-like model which tries to capture some of the special features of the Polish commercial banking sector. The model is then estimated and its tracking power examined. The final section reports some illustrative policy simulations.

The composition of the portfolio

The general background to the banking sector is given in Chapter 2. So here we confine ourselves to the specific issue of the portfolio of the commercial banks. The relevant information is given in Table 3.1 and in Figure 3.1.

Table 3.1 Composition of commercial banks' portfolio in Poland (%)*

Asset/Liability	Dec. 1992	Dec. 1993	Dec. 1994	Dec. 1995
Loans to firms	36.4	33.7	31.6	31.5
Loans to households	1.8	2.4	2.7	3.5
Net foreign assets	11.4	10.4	12.5	7.8
Excess reserves	7.6	7.6	7.2	8.5
Government securities	15.6	19.9	23.8	27.0
Treasury bills	7.8	9.3	10.5	12.2
Treasury bonds (long-term)	6.6	9.6	11.3	11.2
Borrowing from NBP	7.4	6.8	5.8	4.8

*Authors' calculations from the data in NBP bulletins. The ratios are proportions of total gross assets.

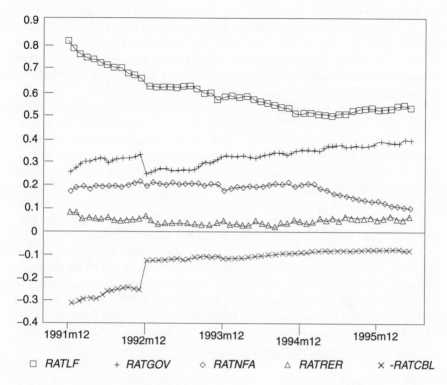

Figure 3.1 Commercial bank portfolio

In view of the fact that the share of loans to the households is very small and the fact that the data on the rates of return on the long-term bonds for the period under study are not available, in Figure 3.1 we do not plot the behaviour of loans to the households or the separate shares of the two types of government securities. It should also be pointed out that since in the estimates the wealth variable which appears in the balance sheet is based on the concept of net assets, that is net of borrowing from the NBP, in the figure, the ratios are proportions of net assets. However, this does not make any appreciable difference to the time path of the different shares reported.

Figure 3.1 presents the ratios: *RLF/RW* (= *RATLF*); *RGOV/RW* (= *RAT-GOV*); *RER/RW* (= *RATRER*); *RFNA/RW* (= *RATNFA*) and − *RCBL/RW* (= −*RATCBL*). Here *RLF* stands for real loans to firms; *RGOV* stands for commercial bank holdings of government securities; *RER* for real excess reserves; *RFNA* for real net foreign assets and *RCBL* for real borrowing from the NBP, shown as a negative asset. *RW* stands for real net wealth. Since the deflator in each case is the consumer price index, these ratios also indicate the nominal ratios as in Table 3.1.

19

Whether we look at the table or the figure, the message is clear. Since the major reforms started, the portfolio of the commercial banks has undergone a very significant change. While the share of loans to firms has continued to shrink, the share of government securities has continued to increase. It is also interesting to note that although the share of loans to the households is minuscule, none the less it has continued to increase steadily. On the other hand, no such clear-cut patterns are discernible in the case of either excess reserves or the borrowings from the NBP. While we do not have the data, as mentioned above, on the rates of return on the long-term bonds, it is still interesting to note that the shares of the two types of securities are almost equal. It would have been interesting to examine the nature of the term structure of interest rates and to see what accounts for this interesting aspect of the portfolio. In short then, there would appear to have been considerable changes in the portfolio composition of the Polish commercial banks, even within a short span of five years, which deserve some explanation.

Before we consider the formal model and its estimates, it may be useful to look at the various rates of return since they are supposed to be the main determinants of the composition. The data on the rate of return on loans to firms (*ADIF*), the rate on government securities (*IG*) and the borrowing rate by the commercial banks on loans from the NBP (*ICB*) are given in Figure 3.2. The rate for loans to firms is net of the default rate. Details about these

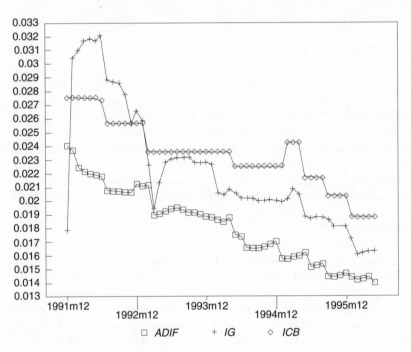

Figure 3.2 Different interest rates

20

variables are provided later in this chapter. Because of the difference in the scale, the rate of return on foreign assets, adjusted for expected exchange rate movements, *(IFO)* is given separately in Figure 3.3.

We can see from Figure 3.2 that the three rates display a strong comovement, particularly since December 1993, while Figure 3.3 shows a much greater volatility in the rate of return on the foreign assets. While not shown, although it can be easily verified from the data Appendix, this volatility is accounted for by the volatility in the rate of exchange rate depreciation. Similarly, while not shown here, but again evident from the data Appendix, the net default rate combines varying behaviour of the rate of default and the gross rate of return on loans to firms. Because of the widely differing behaviour of the components of these two rates, in the next section we will consider two versions of the model, one with a single rate and the other with the separate components.

While we cannot say anything definitive from these figures on the rates, it certainly would seem to be the case that relative movements in the various rates of return had something to do with the observed changes in the shares of the various assets and liability in their portfolio.

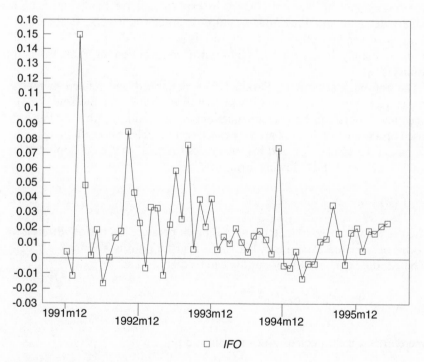

□   *IFO*

Figure 3.3 Foreign yield rate

21

The model

There is a voluminous literature on the role of banks in general and of modelling the banking firm, in particular. It is outside the scope of this paper to give an extensive survey of this literature, but see, for example, Baltensberger (1980), Santomero (1984), Swank (1994) and Thakor (1996). One branch of this literature is very much related to our model, and therefore needs some attention. The model presented in this paper is based on the portfolio balance approach, and hence a brief summary of portfolio balance models applied to the banking firm will be given.

Portfolio balance models assume that a bank is a risk-averse investor, who tries to maximize its expected utility. Mostly, it is assumed that the asset market is perfectly competitive, so that loan rates and deposit rates are given and banks set quantities. However, in some models very much related to the portfolio balance models, some market power for banks is assumed, implying that banks may influence loan and/or deposit rates. Portfolio balance models do not consider the operating expenses of banks, which, according to Baltensberger (1980) is a serious drawback, but according to Santomero (1984) not a serious problem.

In the literature on portfolio balance models applied to the banking firm, two approaches have been taken. The first group of papers, based on Parkin's seminal article of 1970, try to explicitly derive banks' asset and liability demand equations from a choice-theoretic framework. In the other group, however, an optimizing framework is not explicitly used. This second group is mainly based on the well-known contribution of Brainard and Tobin (1968).

The approach set out by Parkin (1970) is applied and refined in many studies (see, e.g., Keating, 1985, van Erp $et\ al.$, 1989 and Sterken, 1991). Since many portfolio balance applications to the banking firm studies are based on Parkin (1970), and are very much comparable, it is useful to explain his model. Parkin (1970), and his successors assumed that banks optimize a utility function of the following form:

$$U(\pi) = a - ce^{-b\pi}; \ b,c > 0; \ u' > 0; \ u'' < 0 \tag{3.1}$$

where a, b and c are parameters and π is profit per decision period. Profit is a stochastic variable. Assuming that the stochastic returns are normally distributed, the expected value of utility can be described as

$$E(U(\pi)) = a - ce^{\left(-\frac{b}{2}E(\pi) + \left(\frac{b}{2}\right)^2 \sigma_\pi^2\right)} \tag{3.2}$$

where $E(\pi)$ is the expected value of profits and

$$\sigma_\pi^2 = E(\pi - E(\pi))^2 \tag{3.3}$$

is the variance of profits. It can now be easily seen that maximizing utility corresponds to maximizing the following expression:

$$M = E(\pi) - \frac{1}{2}b\sigma_\pi^2 \tag{3.4}$$

In the basic model, profits are given by:

$$\pi = W_f - W_0 \tag{3.5}$$

where W_f and W_0 are the values of the portfolio at period $t+f$ and period $t+0$, respectively. They are given by:

$$W_0 = i'v \tag{3.6}$$

$$W_f = (i+m)'v = (i+m+e)'v \tag{3.7}$$

so that

$$E(\pi) = m'v \tag{3.8}$$

where v is a $k \times 1$ vector of assets and liabilities (liabilities are measured as negative assets); $i' = (1, \ldots 1)$; m' is a $1 \times k$ vector of returns on assets, with mean m and variance $E(e_i e_j)$; ' denotes a row vector.

It is worthwhile considering one extension of this basic model. In several studies (e.g., Keating, 1985 and van Erp et al., 1989) adjustment costs are explicitly taken into account in the decision problem. Although the model is still presented in a one period setting, (partial) portfolio adjustments are directly derived from the optimization problem. It is assumed that the bank faces quadratic adjustment costs, so that the expected portfolio return can now be written as:

$$E(\pi) = m'v - 1/2(v - v_0)C(v - v_0) \tag{3.9}$$

where C is a cost matrix, determining costs of selling one asset in order to be able to buy another asset. It is assumed that C is symmetric. The decision problem can now be formulated as follows: choose v in order to maximize

$$M = m'v - \frac{1}{2}(v - v_0)C(v - v_0) - \frac{1}{2}bv'Sv \tag{3.10}$$

subject to

23

$$W_0 = i'v \tag{3.11}$$

where S is the variance–covariance matrix of returns on the assets. The solution to this problem is well-known, and given by (see Courakis, 1988):

$$v = G(m + Cv_0) + HW_0 \tag{3.12}$$

where G is a symmetrical matrix of yield coefficients, depending on the degree of risk aversion (as given by b), the elements of the variance–covariance matrix and the elements of the cost matrix. C is a (non-symmetrical) matrix. H is a column vector, of which the sum of the elements equals one (Engel aggregation). The amount of coefficients to be estimated reduces considerably due to G being symmetrical. It can also be shown that the rows and columns of G total zero, so that the balance sheet is automatically in equilibrium (Cournot aggregation). Moreover, the structure of the matrix is such that an increase in the own rate of return will positively affect the demand for that particular asset. The solution thus implies that, if all interest rates are dependent (non zero covariances), the optimal quantities of assets are functions of all asset returns, of wealth and of all lagged quantities of assets.

The above solution seems to be very appealing. However, Courakis (1988) has severely criticized the choice-theoretic approach of deriving asset demand functions, both on empirical grounds as well as on theoretical grounds. To begin with, in Parkin (1970) and most of its followers, the approach relates to so-called "real" variables. This has basically been done by deflating the vector of assets (v) and wealth (W_0) in the solution above by a deflator, such as the implicit GDP deflator. Courakis (1988) shows that redefining the model in real terms cannot simply be done by deflating the different assets and wealth. If inflation is perfectly anticipated, but not constant in the estimation period, a reinterpretation of the model in *real* magnitudes implies that the composition of the portfolio also depends on the expected inflation rate. An increase in the inflation rate will then act in the same manner as a decrease in absolute risk aversion. Moreover, if the inflation rate is stochastic, and not perfectly anticipated, in addition to the expected inflation rate, the composition of the portfolio will also depend on the variance of the rate of inflation. Finally, in this case some special features of the matrix of coefficients, such as symmetry and homogeneity, will no longer hold and the coefficients for wealth depend on the expected returns. Courakis (1988) also strongly criticizes the followed approach of taking into account adjustment costs. He, for instance, points out that the model including adjustment costs is mis-specified since the adjustment costs are not taken into account in the budget constraint. Moreover, he argues that adjustment costs in practice cannot be described by quadratic costs functions. Finally, Courakis (1988) criticizes the choice-theoretic derivation of asset demands by pointing at empirical evidence which seems to be against some of the major assumptions, such as the existence of symmetry. The symmetry restriction has also been criticized by Roley (1983). He has argued that this restriction has implications for risk aversion criterion, which may not always accord with reality. His testing of the symmetry restrictions in a model of the US Treasury securities market showed that these restrictions were completely rejected.

Due to the critiques of Courakis (1988) and Roley (1983) among others, which strongly question the validity of the choice-theoretic underpinning of the portfolio model, we have decided not to explicitly derive our asset demand equations from an optimizing framework. What we basically do is the following. Based on the model presented above, we assume that desired asset demands depend on all yield rates and on wealth. However, in accordance with empirical evidence we do not assume that the matrix for the interest rates is symmetrical. Moreover, since we consider "real" asset demands, we postulate that the desired demands for "real" assets also depend on an inflation rate. Courakis shows that the inflation rate times the nominal returns on the different assets appears as an argument in the asset demand equations, with the same coefficient as for the different returns (Courakis, 1988, p. 628). However, for reasons of convenience, and since we do not want to make specific restrictions with respect to the coefficients, we simply take into account inflation as an additional argument in the desired demand for assets. We thus follow Parkin (1970) and his successors by assuming that the desired demand for assets depends on wealth and all nominal returns. But, in contrast to the result of the choice theoretic model, we do not assume a symmetrical matrix of coefficients for the yield rates and introduce an inflation rate in the desired asset demand equations. Next, we assume that actual asset demands partially adjust to the desired asset demands. So, we do not explicitly derive adjustments in asset demands from a choice-theoretic framework. In fact, our model is much more in line with the Brainard-Tobin (1968) approach. More specifically, we assume that the asset demand equations of the commercial banks are determined by a multi-asset partial adjustment process (e.g., Owen, 1981). This implies that the change in the different assets can be written as:

$$\Delta a_i = \sum_{j=1}^{n} \lambda_{ij}[a_j{}^* - a_{j,-1}]; \ i = 1, \ldots . n \tag{3.13}$$

where $a_{j,-1}$ is the beginning of period holdings of the ith asset and $a_j{}^*$ is the desired holdings of the ith asset. The vector of assets held by the commercial banks is the same as identified in the previous section, namely,

$$a = (RLF \ RER \ RGOV \ RNFA - RCBL) \tag{3.14}$$

The desired stock of each asset is assumed to depend on all nominal

25

yields, inflation (INFL) and real wealth. As pointed out in the previous section, the model is estimated in two versions as far as the rates of returns on loans to firms and that on net foreign assets are concerned. However, for brevity, we specify only one version for these rates where they are used in their combined form, that is, where the loan rate is adjusted for default rate and the foreign rate for exchange rate depreciation. We can then describe the typical equation for determining desired asset demands as:

$$a_j^* = \alpha_{j0} + \alpha_{j1} + \alpha_{j2}i_g + \alpha_{j3}i_{f0} + \alpha_{j4}i_{cb} +$$

$$\alpha_{j5}INFL + \beta_j RW \quad \text{for} \quad j = 1, \ldots, n. \tag{3.15}$$

We can now derive equations for the change in real asset demands. It is immediately apparent that the flow demand for each asset will depend on all nominal yields, inflation, wealth and the lagged values of all of the dependent variables. In other words, the typical equation will look like:

$$\Delta a_i = \theta_{i0} + \theta_{i1}i_f + \theta_{i2}i_g + \theta_{i3}i_{f0} + \theta_{i4}i_{cb} + \theta_{i5}INFL + \theta_{i6}RW + \theta_{i7}RLF_{-1}$$

$$+ \theta_{i8}RER_{-1} + \theta_{i9}RGOV_{-1} + \theta_{i10}RNFA_{-1} + \theta_{i11}(-RCBL_{-1}) \tag{3.16}$$

where θ_{ij} are the reduced form coefficients being dependent on the adjustment coefficients and/or the structural coefficients. In order to see more explicitly the derivation of θ_{ij} and the adding up constraint of **(3.16)**, we can take an illustrative example with only two assets.

Let the two assets be a_1 and a_2 and their respective rates of return i_1 and i_2 and let wealth be defined as $a_1 + a_2 = W$. Then the equations corresponding to **(3.15)** for these assets can be written as

$$a_1^* = \alpha_{11}i_1 + \alpha_{12}i_2 + \beta_1 W \tag{3.17}$$

$$a_2^* = \alpha_{21}i_1 + \alpha_{22}i_2 + \beta_2 W \tag{3.18}$$

Substituting **(3.17)** and **(3.18)** into **(3.13)** and collecting terms, we get

$$\Delta a_1 = (\lambda_{11}\alpha_{11} + \lambda_{12}\alpha_{21})i_1 + (\lambda_{11}\alpha_{12} + \lambda_{12}\alpha_{22})i_2$$

$$+ (\lambda_{11}\beta_1 + \lambda_{12}\beta_2)W - \lambda_{11}a_{1,-1} - \lambda_{12}a_{2,-1} \tag{3.19}$$

$$\Delta a_2 = (\lambda_{21}\alpha_{11} + \lambda_{22}\alpha_{21})i_1 + (\lambda_{21}\alpha_{12} + \lambda_{22}\alpha_{22})i_2$$

$$+ (\lambda_{21}\beta_1 + \lambda_{22}\beta_2)W - \lambda_{21}a_{1,-1} - \lambda_{22}a_{2,-1} \tag{3.20}$$

Equations **(3.19)** and **(3.20)** are of the form **(3.16)** where the reduced form coefficients depend on the structural coefficients λ_{ij} and α_{ij}. In order to derive the adding-up restrictions, equations **(3.19)** and **(3.20)** must be solved for a_1 and a_2. This will lead to:

$$a_1 = (\lambda_{11}\alpha_{11} + \lambda_{12}\alpha_{21})i_1 + (\lambda_{11}\alpha_{12} + \lambda_{12}\alpha_{22})i_2$$
$$+ (\lambda_{11}\beta_1 + \lambda_{12}\beta_2)W - (1 - \lambda_{11})a_{1,-1} - \lambda_{12}a_{2,-1} \qquad (3.21)$$

$$a_2 = (\lambda_{21}\alpha_{11} + \lambda_{22}\alpha_{21})i_1 + (\lambda_{21}\alpha_{12} + \lambda_{22}\alpha_{22})i_2$$
$$+ (\lambda_{21}\beta_1 + \lambda_{22}\beta_2)W - \lambda_{21}a_{1,-1} + (1 - \lambda_{22})a_{2,-1} \qquad (3.22)$$

The adding up restrictions from **(3.21)** and **(3.22)** imply that:

$$\alpha_{11}(\lambda_{11} + \lambda_{21}) + \alpha_{21}(\lambda_{12} + \lambda_{22}) = 0$$

$$\alpha_{12}(\lambda_{11} + \lambda_{21}) + \alpha_{22}(\lambda_{12} + \lambda_{22}) = 0 \qquad (3.23)$$

$$(1 - \lambda_{11}) - \lambda_{21} = 0 \qquad (3.24)$$

$$-\lambda_{12} + (1 - \lambda_{22}) = 0 \qquad (3.25)$$

$$(\lambda_{11}\beta_1 + \lambda_{12}\beta_2) + (\lambda_{21}\beta_1 + \lambda_{22}\beta_2) = 1 \qquad (3.26)$$

The adding-up restrictions are imposed in the estimation procedure.

For purposes of estimation, we estimate equation **(3.16)** in two forms. First, as mentioned before, we define the rates of return on loans to firms adjusted for default rates and adjust the return on foreign assets by the exchange rate depreciation of the domestic currency. In the second version, these two rates are replaced by their constituent components.

Estimation results

This section presents the estimation results of our theoretical model as presented in Section 3.2. Before describing the regression results, a short explanation of some of the yield variables used in the estimates is necessary. With respect to the loan rate for firms, the NBP (Central Bank of Poland) presents figures for interest rates on credits with lowest risk rates, bills of exchange discount rates and rates on overdue credits (these are also called prime rates, discount rates and default rates). In principle, all rates might be used as proxies for the lending rate for firms in our model. However, since we have explicitly taken into account default rates in the estimation process, we had a preference for using lending rates on credits with lowest risk rates. In the final estimates, these rates are used as proxies for the lending rates on loans for firms. In alternative estimates, we have also experimented with lending rates on overdue credits and with average rates (consisting of lending rates on credits with lowest risk and lending rates on overdue credits). It appeared that significance levels were almost the same for all lending rates used, which is of course not surprising if we take into account the existence of strong multicollinearity between the different lending rates for firms. Only the coefficients differ somewhat for the alternative lending rates. With respect to the lending rate for commercial banks on loans from the central bank, in principle three rates can be used: the refinancing rate, the rediscount rate and the Lombard rate. These rates are all used by the Central Bank of Poland as part of its monetary policy. In the estimates we have experimented with all three rates. Here also the estimation results were relatively insensitive to the particular central bank lending rate used. In the final estimates we have approximated the lending rate on loans from the central bank by the unweighted average of the reference rate, the Lombard rate and the rediscount rate. With respect to the yield on government securities, the NBP gives yields on treasury bills and yields on treasury bonds. Either a weighted average of treasury bill yields and treasury bond yields or separate yields on the two types of securities would have been preferable. However, data for treasury bond yields were, for most years in our estimation period, lacking, so we have had to use treasury bill yields as proxies for the yield on government securities. With respect to the treasury bill yields, we have experimented with 8-week bill yields, 26-week bill yields, 52-week bill yields and averages of these three treasury bills yields. The results for all of these rates were almost identical. In the final estimates the 8-week treasury bill yields are used. With respect to the foreign interest rate, we had several options. The rate used in the estimates is the US deposit rate, which is published by the IMF. The default rates used in the estimates refer to the percentage of bank claims on businesses in bad financial standing of total corporate outstanding debt to 15 or 16 most important banks. These figures are given, until the end of 1995, in the descriptive part of the information bulletins of the NBP, under the heading businesses in bad financial standing. Expected inflation rates and expected devaluations are proxied by actual inflation rates (calculated from consumer price indices) and actual rates of depreciation (calculated from free-market exchange rates).

In fact, all yield rates used in portfolio models refer to *expected* yield rates. Since these rates are not observable, we had to make a decision about the way expectations are formed in our model. We decided to be very pragmatic on this point. In the estimates we experimented with actual rates, one period ahead rates, one period lagged rates, two period lagged rates and some average of these rates. It turned out that in almost all cases the one period lagged rates gave the best results. Hence, almost all expected yield rates are proxied by the actual one period lagged rates. For some rates, however, the actual rates are used (see explanation below the tables).

We also had to make a decision with respect to the estimation method. In line with usual practice for estimating portfolio models, we have estimated the model by using the generalized least squares method of the Zellner type, or in other words Zellner's seemingly unrelated regression method. This method gives the same results as the ordinary least squares method in the case where all equations have the same regressors. However, if some regressors are deleted from one or more of the equations, which will often be the case due to multicollinearity problems, Zellner's results differ from the OLS results. To circumvent the problem of the singular variance–covariance matrix of disturbances when all equations are estimated simultaneously, one of the equations is deleted from the system. In our estimates, the equation for net foreign assets is deleted from the system. The coefficients for this equation can be obtained by considering the adding-up restrictions.

Finally, a word on the estimation period is in order. It appeared to be virtually impossible to use time series data for a long period, say starting in the 1980s or the 1970s. First, the collapse of the communist system probably caused a serious structural break, which may have affected the behaviour of commercial banks. The Lucas critique may be a serious problem when the equations are estimated using data from the period before and after the communist breakdown. Second, even if this is not considered to be a major problem, using data from the 1980s and the 1970s is troublesome since data for these periods are extremely unreliable and often not available. Moreover, during 1991 the system of accounts for most monetary variables was changed, so that series on monetary variables before and after 1991 are not comparable. For these reasons we have used data for the period beginning December 1991 until May 1996 (the latest date available to us when we did the estimates). In order to have enough degrees of freedom, we have used monthly data in the estimates. We recognize that monthly data may contain too much noise or suffer from excessive errors of measurement with the well-known consequences for the estimated coefficients, but given the shortage of the data, there really wasn't much of an option.

Our estimation procedure was as follows. We first started by estimating the full model, for different assumptions with respect to the lags. The estimation results for the full model are given in Table 3.2. Next, we estimated the full model, in which the components of the yields on the loans to firms and the yield on the foreign assets are entered as separate arguments. These results are given in Table 3.3. Finally, after deleting variables from the system which had the theoretically wrong sign, we reestimated the whole system, and then omitting variables with highly insignificant coefficients, we arrived at a preferred set of estimates.

A brief discussion of these results is now in order. Regardless of the table we consider, the coefficient of wealth remains relatively robust. The results accord with expectations with regard to the signs of the lagged variables. In most cases these coefficients are significant. Turning our attention to the most important aspect of the estimates, namely, the signs and the significance of the coefficients of the various yields, we consider the estimates in Table 3.4.

Table 3.2 Full model estimation results: combined yield rates

	ΔRL_f	ΔRER	$\Delta RGOV$	$-\Delta RCBL$
ifo	7359	12578	−13782	−5655
	(0.97)	(1.24)	(−0.79)	(−0.36)
adi_f	610864	−858557	−939491	917533
	(1.52)	(−1.61)	(−1.02)	(1.11)
i_{cb}	−256335	1167112	631898	−1183666
	(−0.76)	(2.62)	(0.82)	(−1.71)
i_g	96362	−169940	164379	85811
	(0.87)	(−1.15)	(0.64)	(0.37)
INFL	−135001	82854	−19582	119242
	(−5.51)	(2.54)	(−0.35)	(2.36)
RW	0.169	0.260	0.176	0.365
	(3.95)	(4.58)	(1.79)	(4.14)
$RL_{f,-1}$	−0.252	−0.290	0.218	−0.641
	(−3.41)	(−2.96)	(1.28)	(−4.20)
$RGOV_{-1}$	−0.133	−0.184	−0.258	−0.333
	(−2.36)	(−2.46)	(−1.98)	(−2.86)
$-RCBL_{-1}$	−0.127	−0.292	0.049	−0.530
	(−2.64)	(−4.54)	(0.44)	(−5.31)
$RNFA_{-1}$	−0.158	−0.529	−0.002	−0.303
	(−1.85)	(−4.64)	(−0.01)	(−1.71)
RER_{-1}	−0.052	−0.898	0.064	−0.092
	(−0.64)	(−8.43)	(0.34)	(−0.56)
Constant	4898	6735	−58457	36133
	(0.31)	(0.32)	(−1.62)	(1.11)
R^2	0.78	0.66	0.25	0.43
DW	2.60	2.13	2.00	1.90
Obs.	53	53	53	53
SD DEPV	3149.127	3315.983	3891.912	4005.002
SQ RES	1.12E+08	1.97E+08	5.93E+08	4.76E+08
MEAN DV	−536.0776	−3.931336	1058.078	905.9672
SE Reg	1649.932	2191.638	3802.015	3408.466

Note: In estimates all yields are current values, except for inflation which is one period lagged. R^2 is *R*-squared; DW is Durbin-Watson Statistic; obs. = number of observations. ifo = foreign interest rate corrected for expected depreciation of home currency; adi_f = after default loan rate for firms, calculated as (i-default)*i_f; SD DEPV = standard deviation of dependent variable; SQ RES = sum of squared residuals; MEAN DV = mean of dependent variable; SE Reg = standard error of regression. Variables in "real" terms are calculated by deflating the corresponding variables in nominal terms (see Table A6.1.1) by the price index (see Table A6.1.2).

The results are surprisingly informative. Thus, the own rate of return for loans to firms is highly significant and of correct sign. Similar is the case for the rate of return on government securities in the equation for this asset. The same holds true for the central bank's borrowing rate. In short, then, the own rates of return seem to perform quite well. The cross-effects are also interesting. One interesting result is that relating to the effect of the default rate on loans to firms. We saw in Chapter 2 that the problem of bad loans was

Table 3.3 Full model estimation results: separated yields

	ΔRL_f	ΔRER	$\Delta RGOV$	$-\Delta RCBL$
PER	2040	14903	−13403	−10355
	(0.26)	(1.45)	(−0.81)	(−0.86)
i_e	−632321	−1273905	3650777	−3484428
	(−1.07)	(−2.53)	(2.88)	(−3.42)
i_f	499787	−1093479	−169044	326604
	(1.56)	(−2.53)	(−0.24)	(0.59)
i_{cb}	−349822	1136175	−955141	797944
	(−0.89)	(2.17)	(−1.14)	(1.18)
i_g	90480	59996	1228324	−1477829
	(0.39)	(0.19)	(2.49)	(−3.00)
DEF	−47134	−7976	−9414	−2497
	(−2.80)	(−0.35)	(−0.26)	(−0.86)
INFL	−134848	75421	−47275	161782
	(−5.63)	(2.35)	(−0.92)	(3.92)
RW	0.164	0.235	0.119	0.430
	(3.91)	(4.19)	(1.32)	(5.97)
$RL_{f,-1}$	−0.314	−0.369	0.241	−0.627
	(−4.05)	(−3.55)	(1.45)	(−4.09)
$RGOV_{-1}$	−0.102	−0.141	−0.291	−0.312
	(−1.88)	(−1.91)	(−2.50)	(−3.34)
$-RCBL_{-1}$	−0.146	−0.300	0.235	−0.759
	(−2.87)	(−4.31)	(2.13)	(−8.58)
$RNFA_{-1}$	−0.039	−0.400	−0.010	−0.283
	(−0.41)	(−3.09)	(−0.049)	(−1.70)
RER_{-1}	−0.041	−0.928	−0.189	0.178
	(−0.50)	(−8.50)	(−1.08)	(1.27)
Constant	21601	28624	−44139	11997
	(1.28)	(1.27)	(−1.22)	(0.41)
R^2	0.76	0.69	0.42	0.65
DW	2.45	2.07	2.07	1.82
Obs.	52	52	52	52
SD DEPV	2856.679	3347.254	3920.815	4043.938
SQ RES	98667372	1.77E+08	4.55E+08	2.93E+08
MEAN DV	−346.0766	7.644269	1021.781	901.4186
SE Reg	1611.369	2157.746	3458.896	2775.800

Note: in estimates i_f, i_{cb}, i_g and PER are one period lagged. DEF is two period lagged. R^2 is R-squared; DW is Durbin-Watson Statistic; obs. = number of observations. SD DEPV = standard deviation of dependent variable; SQ RES = sum of squared residuals; MEAN DV = mean of dependent variable; SE Reg = standard error of regression. Variables in "real" terms are calculated by deflating the corresponding variables in nominal terms (see Table A6.1.1) by the price index (see Table A6.1.2).

pervasive in the economies in transition and that the banks were reluctant to provide loans to firms keeping the rate of return on such loans constant. This hypothesis would appear to be confirmed. The variable DEF is negative and highly significant. Interestingly enough, the same variable, though with the correct sign, is statistically insignificant in the equation for the demand for

Table 3.4 Preferred estimation results

	ΔRLF	ΔRER	$\Delta RGOV$	$-\Delta RCBL$
PER				−11937
				(−1.91)
i_e				−1738423
				(−3.88)
i_f	836769		−891342	
	(3.24)		(−2.84)	
i_{cb}	−553534			826730
	(−2.43)			(2.54)
i_g			1052396	−1284432
			(3.22)	(−4.05)
DEF	−44248		−15288	
	(−3.56)		(−0.94)	
INFL	−151693	88856		124891
	(−8.60)	(3.46)		(4.92)
RW	0.168	0.303	0.102	0.405
	(5.46)	(5.64)	(2.43)	(7.85)
$RL_{f,-1}$	−0.228	−0.319		−0.482
	(−5.87)	(−5.38)		(−8.49)
$RGOV_{-1}$	−0.093	−0.175	−0.219	−0.362
	(−2.09)	(−2.89)	(−2.63)	(−5.03)
$-RCBL_{-1}$	−0.140	−0.357	0.184	−0.697
	(−3.33)	(−6.68)	(1.95)	(−8.38)
$RNFA_{-1}$		−0.444		−0.261
		(−6.46)		(−7)
RER_{-1}		−0.873		
		(−10.34)		
R^2	0.75	0.60	0.29	0.60
DW	2.47	2.11	1.92	1.80
Obs.	52	52	52	52
SD DEPV	2856.679	3315.983	3920.815	4043.938
SQ RES	105E+08	2.28E+08	5.53E+08	3.37E+08
MEAN DV	−346.0766	−3.931336	1021.781	901.4186
SE Reg	1544.028	2226.288	3468.544	2834.250

Note: in estimates i_f, i_{cb}, i_g and PER are one period lagged. DEF is two period lagged. R^2 is *R*-squared; DW is Durbin-Watson Statistic; obs. = number of observations. SD DEPV = standard deviation of dependent variable; SQ RES = sum of squared residuals; MEAN DV= mean of dependent variable; SE Reg = standard error of regression. Variables in "real" terms are calculated by deflating the corresponding variables in nominal terms (see Table A6.1.1) by the price index (see Table A6.1.2).

government securities, suggesting that the banks do not have the same negative attitude towards the government in terms of its solvability.

What is most surprising about these results is that they are so promising when we keep in mind the fact that they are really based on a period of less than five years. It would appear that the commercial banks in Poland have learnt fast in terms of reacting to market forces when managing their balance sheets.

Tracking ability of the estimated model

In the estimated model of the last section we did not pay much attention to the "fit" of the model. A better check as to whether the estimated model provides a good fit to the data is to see how it would forecast the time path of the levels, the flows and the shares of the various assets and the liability within the sample period. There are generally two types of forecasts done for such purposes: static and dynamic. In the former, the actual values of the independent as well as the lagged dependent variables are used. In the latter, while the actual values of the independent or the exogenous variables are used, for the lagged dependent variables, except for the first observation, the subsequent values are those predicted by the model in the previous period. It is clear from this brief description that the latter provides a stiffer test of the model to track the time path of the dependent variables because in this case there is the possibility of errors being cumulated and thus compounded. Consequently, in this section we report the results of dynamic simulations.

We simulate the time path of the stocks, that is the levels, the flows, that is the change in stocks and the ratio of the various assets and the liability. The simulations are performed with a simulation package developed at the University of Groningen, the GUESS (Groningen University Econometric Simulation System) programme (Kroonenberg, 1991). GUESS provides some test statistics by which the model behaviour can be tested. For the *ex post* simulation technique it compares the actual and simulated series of a certain variable by calculating Theil's inequality coefficient and the coefficient of determination (R^2). Theil's coefficient (TC) measures whether the shape of the simulated series and the actual series is similar. It is calculated as:

$$TC = \frac{\sqrt{\Sigma \Delta r_t^2}}{\sqrt{\Sigma \Delta o_t^2} + \sqrt{\Sigma \Delta s_t^2}} \tag{3.27}$$

where $r =$ the residual; o is the actual value and s the simulated variable. Theil's coefficient falls between one and zero. A perfect fit implies that the coefficient becomes zero. There are no formal rules with respect to the value of Theil's coefficient by which one can decide whether the model behaves satisfactorily or not. However, Kuipers *et al.* (1988) argue, by using a rule of thumb, that a Theil's coefficient below 0.75 is satisfactory, a coefficient below 0.50 is reasonable, and a coefficient below 0.25 is good. The coefficient of determination is calculated as:

$$R^2 = 1 - \frac{\Sigma r_t^2}{\Sigma (o_t - o_{avg})^2} \tag{3.28}$$

where o_{avg} denotes the average of the series. Note that the R^2 calculated in simulations, in contrast to the R^2 calculated in regressions, may become negative.

Table 3.5 shows the forecasts for the flows, the stocks and the ratios. Looking at the R^2, we can see that, as one might expect, the levels are forecasted better than the flows. The ratios on the other hand are also forecasted reasonably well except for the free reserves where the R^2 is only 0.57.

The graphic representations of all three types of the series are not presented. We confine ourselves only to the shares, particularly because in this chapter we are interested only in finding out how the portfolio composition changes in response to some of the decision variables and not in the absolute values of the stocks or flows. These time paths of the various shares are given in Figures 3.4 to 3.8.

Figure 3.4 clearly shows that the model very accurately traces the behaviour of the share of loans to the firms during the sample period. With regard to the share of borrowing from the NBP, shown in Figure 3.5, the tracking is somewhat choppy in 1993 but quite satisfactory thereafter – particularly since January 1995. As suggested by the value of the R^2 in Table 3.5, the model does not track that well the time path of excess reserves as can be seen from Figure 3.6. But even in this case the directions of the changes are predicted reasonably well. The share of the government securities in the

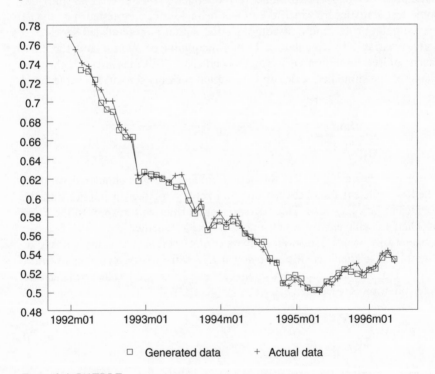

Figure 3.4 RATRLF

34

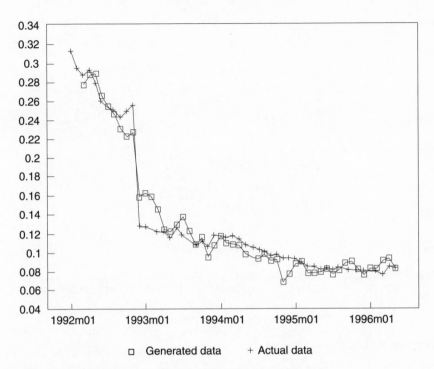

Figure 3.5 RATRCBL

Table 3.5 Test results for dynamic simulations

	R^2	TC
DRLF	0.724	0.332
DRER	0.438	0.438
DRGOV	0.178	0.759
DRCBL	0.419	0.447
DRNFA	0.329	0.626
RLF	0.955	0.277
RER	0.622	0.446
RGOV	0.933	0.613
RCBL	0.939	0.441
RNFA	0.872	0.470
RATRLF	0.992	0.250
RATRER	0.570	0.465
RATRGOV	0.827	0.530
RATRCBL	0.959	0.359
RATRNFA	0.911	0.469

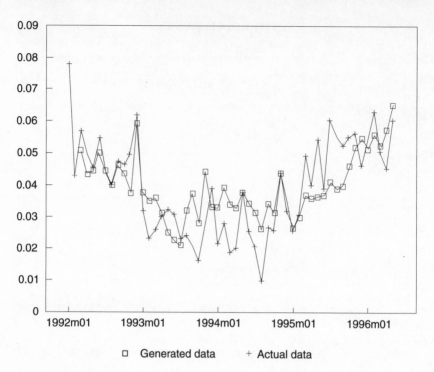

Figure 3.6 RATRER

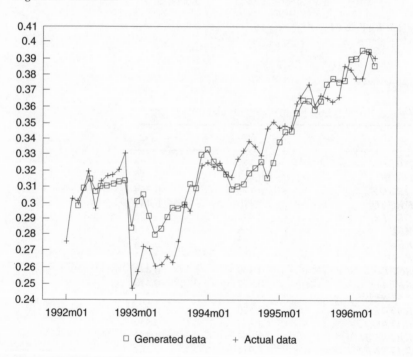

Figure 3.7 RATRGOV

portfolio is also tracked well except for the period 1993–94, as shown in Figure 3.7. What is particularly remarkable about this figure is that it does such a good job, even though we had to proxy the rate of return on the two types of securities by the return on the t-bill rate only. A possible reason may be that the two rates, for the short period for which we have the data on them, moved very closely together. Finally, Figure 3.8 shows the time path of the share of the net foreign assets. Recall that the estimates of this equation were obtained from the adding-up restrictions. This means that the burden of all the mistakes in the other equations falls on the estimates for this asset. The outcome is truly remarkable in this case, particularly since 1994.

On the whole, then, based on the estimates of the model in the previous section as well as the dynamic forecasts of this section, we are inclined to conclude that the model of this chapter provides a reasonable explanation of the portfolio behaviour of the commercial banks in Poland.

Illustrative policy simulations

Although the model in this chapter is only one component of the complete model to be presented in Chapter 6, none the less it is interesting to see how, even in a partial equilibrium framework, the composition of the commercial banks' portfolio may respond to the various rates of return. In this section we carry out a few simulations to examine this issue.

Our simulation strategy is as follows. We start with a base simulation in which all of the exogenous variables to run the model are set at their May 1996 value during the whole simulation period. Next, we simulate the model by increasing the value of the exogenous variables one at a time. In the figures we plot the deviations from the base simulation. The meaning of the figures is straightforward. If the deviations are positive then it implies that the variable under consideration is positively affected by the change in the exogenous variable. The graphic representation again refers to the behaviour of the shares. We present the time path of the (change in) shares of the different assets of the commercial banking sector in a single figure.

We present simulations with respect to an increase in i_f, rate on loans to firms (Figure 3.9); i_{cb} the borrowing rate by commercial banks on loans from the NBP (Figure 3.10) and i_g, the rate on government securities (Figure 3.11). For all cases we have assessed the effect of a 25 per cent increase in these rates. Given that we are dealing only with a partial equilibrium framework in this chapter, we do not wish to carry the interpretation of the simulations reported too far. Therefore we offer only a brief discussion. The first striking result is the effect of own rates of return on the shares of the asset concerned. Thus, in Figure 3.9, an increase in i_f leads to an increase in the share of loans to firms, *ceteris paribus*, as one would expect. Similarly, Figure 3.10 suggests that the share of borrowing from the NBP decreases in response to

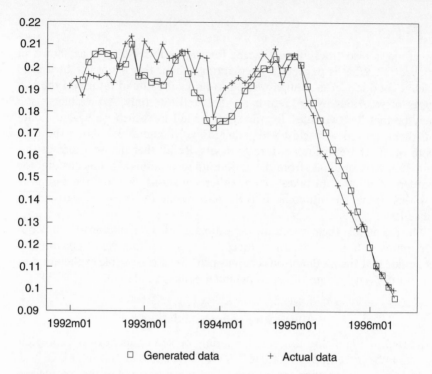

□ Generated data   + Actual data

Figure 3.8 RATRNFA

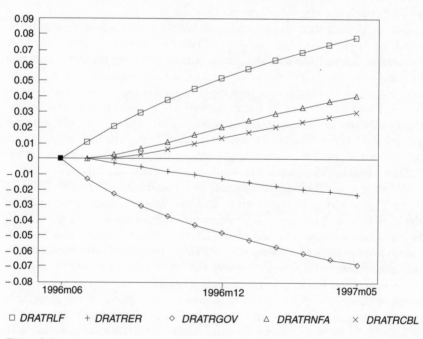

□ *DRATRLF*   + *DRATRER*   ◇ *DRATRGOV*   △ *DRATRNFA*   × *DRATRCBL*

Figure 3.9 i_f

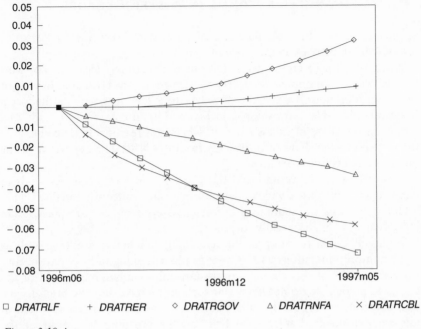

□ *DRATRLF*　　+ *DRATRER*　　◇ *DRATRGOV*　　△ *DRATRNFA*　　× *DRATRCBL*

Figure 3.10 i_{cb}

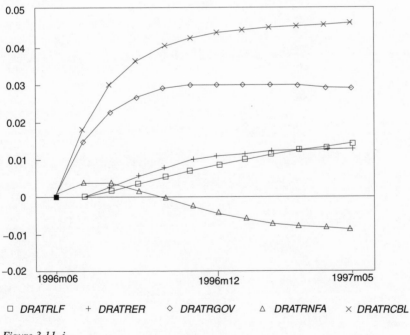

□ *DRATRLF*　　+ *DRATRER*　　◇ *DRATRGOV*　　△ *DRATRNFA*　　× *DRATRCBL*

Figure 3.11 i_g

an increase in i_{cb}. Finally, the share of government securities increases in response to an increase in their rate of return.

When we turn to cross effects, the outcomes are less clearcut, not least because we did not impose symmetry restrictions on the estimates. In view of these considerations, we confine ourselves to a few observations that seem intuitively plausible. For example, in Figure 3.9, an increase in i_f leads to a decline in the share of excess reserves, which is a reasonable outcome, as is the increase in the share of borrowing from the NBP. The behaviour of the other two assets is less obvious.

From Figure 3.10, we find that the share of real excess reserves tends to increase as i_{cb} increases, which is again a plausible outcome. Finally, Figure 3.11 suggests that the share held in foreign assets declines in response to an increase in i_g: again, not really surprising.

We could similarly interpret the remaining simulation results as well as conduct more simulations with respect to the remaining rates of return. But, since the model of this chapter constitutes only one building block for the complete model, we do not carry out such an exercise. But the brief discussion above does suggest that the framework and the estimates reported in this chapter do shed interesting light on the portfolio behaviour of the commercial banks in Poland.

4

HOUSEHOLDS

In this chapter we turn our attention to the household sector of the Polish economy. The basic format of the chapter is the same as that of the commercial banking chapter. We first look at the major changes which have taken place in the portfolio composition of the Polish households since the beginning of the reform period. This is followed by specification of a model which explains both consumption/saving and the portfolio selection decisions, and the implications of this integrated approach are brought out against the sequential approach. A detailed discussion of the data used to estimate the model is then undertaken, followed by the estimates of the model and their discussion. This chapter is then concluded with an examination of the tracking ability of the estimated model and some illustrative policy simulations.

The composition of the household portfolio

The detailed data and the implications of the distinction between the zloty-denominated and the foreign currency-denominated deposits are discussed in the following sections. Here we present some summary statistics and a few figures to highlight some of the major changes that have taken place in the portfolio composition since the beginning of the reform process. Table 4.1 gives percentage holdings of the six main assets in net worth for four benchmark dates. Figure 4.1 gives the ratios of foreign currency deposits to wealth ($RATRHFD$); ratios of foreign currency time deposits to wealth ($RATRHFTD$); the ratios of zloty demand deposits to wealth ($RATRHD$); the ratios of zloty time deposits to wealth ($RATRHTD$); and the ratios of currency to wealth ($RATRCUR$) and Figure 4.2 plots the ratios of net other assets to wealth ($RATRHNOA$) and the ratios of net foreign assets to wealth ($RATRHNFA$) for the period December 1991 to May 1996 on a monthly basis.

From Table 4.1 we can see a number of interesting features. The importance of currency in the portfolio has steadily declined, as have the holdings of foreign currency-denominated demand deposits. On the other hand, the relative importance of zloty-denominated over foreign currency-denominated

41

time deposits has gone up. The changing share of net foreign assets is also interesting. From 28 per cent in December 1992 to –9 per cent in May 1996 is quite an extraordinary change. This move away from foreign assets and foreign currency-denominated deposits is one of the more important changes in the portfolio composition of the Polish households. One of the aims of the model in the next section and in policy simulation later on is to capture the implications of these changes. The statistical changes discussed above can also be seen in greater detail in Figures 4.1 and 4.2. The seemingly strange behaviour of net other assets and net foreign assets should not be a surprise given the way they have been calculated, as explained below.

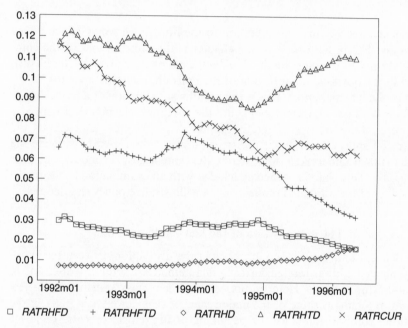

Figure 4.1 Portfolio: households

Table 4.1 Composition of household portfolio (%)

	Dec. 1992	Dec. 1993	Dec. 1994	Dec. 1995	May 1996
RATRHFD	2.5	3	3.1	2.1	1.8
RATRHFTD	6.4	7.1	6.1	3.9	3.3
RATRHD	0.7	0.9	1	1.4	1.8
RATRHTD	11.8	9.7	8.8	10.8	11.1
RATRCUR	9.8	8	6.5	6.9	6.4
RATRHNFA	27.9	13.1	–1.2	–7.3	–9.1
RATRHNOA	40.8	58.1	75.6	82.2	84.7

Source: Calculated from data Appendix

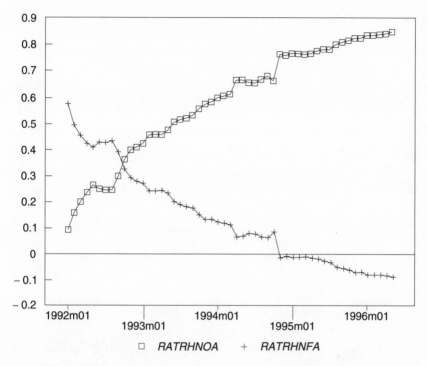

Figure 4.2 Portfolio: households

Having looked at some of the major changes in the portfolio composition of the Polish households, it is instructive to look at the behaviour of the rates of return on the various assets. Since we have already presented the data on the US interest rates, the depreciation rates and inflation in the last chapter, here we present only four rates. Since in the estimates we take after-tax rate of returns into account, the rates refer to after-tax nominal rates. Figure 4.3 gives the rates on the two foreign-denominated deposits and the zloty demand deposits (*ATIFD*, *ATIFTD* and *ATID*). The after tax rate of return on zloty time deposits (*ATITD*) is given in Figure 4.4. This is for reasons of scale. If we plot all four rates in one diagram, we cannot see the differences between the four rates. It would obviously be wrong to draw any major conclusions about the effects of the differences in the relative rates of return on the changing portfolio composition observed above; none the less, it is interesting to note that some of the changes in the portfolio composition do seem to correspond with the changes in the relative rates of return. But a more appropriate inference is possible only from formal estimates of a model. This task is the subject matter of the next section.

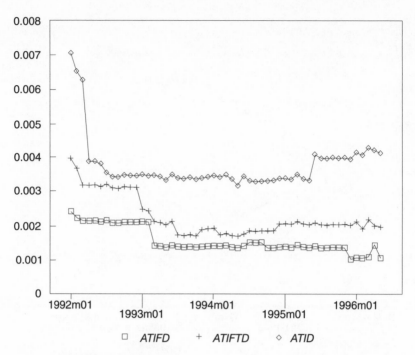

Figure 4.3 After-tax interest rates

The model

We start the description of the model for the household sector by presenting the budget constraint. The real budget constraint reads as:

$$Y - C = \Delta RHD + \Delta RHTD + \Delta RHFD + \Delta RHFTD + \Delta RHNFA +$$

$$\Delta RCUR + \Delta RHNOA \tag{4.1}$$

where RHD = real stock of zloty demand deposits; $RHTD$ = real stock of zloty time deposits; $RHFD$ = real stock of foreign currency demand deposits held at Polish commercial banks; $RHFTD$ = real stock of foreign currency time deposits held at Polish commercial banks; $RCUR$ = real stock of currency; $RHNFA$ = real stock of net foreign assets; $RHNOA$ = real stock of net other assets; Y = real disposable income; C = real consumption and Δ = a change in a variable. The H in the variables refers to "households".

The budget constraint shows that households use their income for consumption, as well as for accumulating time and demand deposits, denominated in zloty and foreign currencies, currency, foreign assets and net other assets. Bank loans to households are not taken into account due to their

44

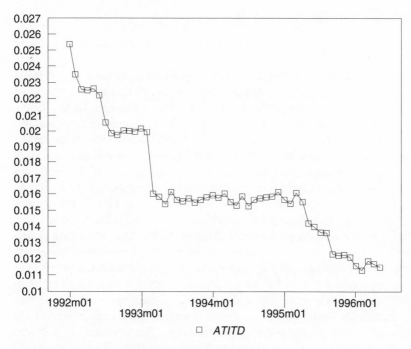

Figure 4.4 After-tax time deposit rates

relative unimportance in the households' portfolio. The distinction between deposits denominated in zloty and in foreign currencies is one particular feature of the budget constraint worth considering in more detail. One particular feature of the Polish financial system is the importance of foreign currency-denominated deposits held at commercial banks. Since 1967 Polish citizens have been allowed to hold foreign currency-denominated assets in Polish commercial bank accounts. These deposits mainly serve as an inflation hedge. The Polish authorities even encouraged the holdings of foreign assets as they needed foreign exchange to pay for international debt services. Zloty and foreign currency-denominated deposits have become important substitutes, and this does have important implications for the Polish government's monetary policy. Since the government only partly controls the domestic money stock, the existence of foreign currency-denominated deposits complicates monetary policy. Moreover, the possibility of using the inflation tax measure is reduced if households hold foreign currency-denominated deposits. The other parts of the budget constraint are straightforward, and hence do not need additional explanation.

In line with the approach for the commercial banking sector, asset demand equations for the household sector are derived by a multivariable adjustment process. The change in the different assets is thus written:

$$\Delta a_i = \sum_{j=1}^{n} \lambda_{ij}[a_j^* - a_{j,-1}] \tag{4.2}$$

where $a_{j,-1}$ is the beginning-of-period holdings of the ith asset and a_j^* is the desired holding of the ith asset.

A particular feature of the model we use here is that we consider the portfolio allocation and consumption-savings decision simultaneously. In most portfolio models, like the celebrated model of Brainard and Tobin (1968), households first make a decision with respect to consumption and savings, given the total level of end of period wealth. Next, households decide on the allocation of wealth amongst different assets. Hence, the portfolio-allocation and consumption-savings decisions are separated. Purvis (1978) proposes a model in which the consumption-savings decision and the portfolio allocation decision are integrated. A special feature of his model is that current wealth does not affect the asset-demand equations. This is based on the idea that it is the composition of wealth instead of the level of wealth which determines the optimal decision paths.[1] However, as explained by Smith (1978), Purvis's approach (1978) is overrestrictive in the sense that it assumes that current wealth does not affect desired asset holdings. Smith (1978) argues that there may exist a certain hierarchy of decisions, in the sense that some variables possibly affect the consumption-savings decision, but do not directly affect the portfolio-allocation decision. These variables, however, indirectly affect the portfolio-allocation decision via their effect on wealth. If current wealth is not an argument in the desired asset demand equations, these indirect effects are neglected. The obvious solution to this problem is to include current wealth in the equations for the desired asset demands.

Therefore, we follow the portfolio model as developed by Owen (1981). Her model embodies the models in line with Brainard–Tobin, Purvis and Smith, and hence is as general as possible. In our view this approach is preferable to an approach in which one of the specific versions of the portfolio models is used, since these versions should at the least be treated as testable hypotheses.

The desired stock of assets of the household sector is assumed to be of the following form:

$$a_j^* = \zeta_{j,0} + \zeta_{j,1}Y + \zeta_{j,2}RHNW + \zeta_{j,3}IFTD(1 - htaxr)$$
$$+ \zeta_{j,4}IFD(1 - htaxr) + \zeta_{j,5}ID(1 - htaxr) + \zeta_{j,6}IFO(1 - htaxr)$$
$$+ \zeta_{j,7}\pi + \zeta_{j,8}pe + \zeta_{j,9}ITD(1 - htaxr) \tag{4.3}$$

where $RHNW$ is real net wealth; ID is the (zloty) demand deposit rate; ITD is the (zloty) time deposit rate; IFD is the demand deposit rate for foreign currency-denominated demand deposits; $IFTD$ is the time deposit rate on foreign currency-denominated time deposits; IFO is the foreign interest rate and $htaxr$ is the personal tax rate.

Equation **(4.3)** needs some explanation. The asset demands are assumed to depend on the different (nominal) yield indicators. Currency and net other assets are assumed not to be remunerated. Net of tax rates of return are introduced to allow for the fact that households consider after-tax returns in their portfolio allocation procedure. In line with the approach followed in the previous chapter, nominal rates and inflation are treated as separate arguments. The same applies to the foreign nominal interest rate and the expected relative change in the exchange rate. Real net wealth is introduced in order to be able to take account of the indirect effects of changes in wealth, as explained above.

A typical asset demand equation for households will now look like as follows:

$$\Delta a_i = \theta_{i,0} + \theta_{i,1} Y + \theta_{i,2} RHNW + \theta_{i,3} IFTD(1 - htaxr) + \theta_{i,4} IFD(1 - htaxr)$$
$$+ \theta_{i,5} ID(1 - htaxr) + \theta_{i,6} ITD(1 - htaxr) + \theta_{i,7} IFO(1 - htaxr)$$
$$+ \theta_{i,8}\pi + \theta_{i,9} pe + \theta_{i,10} RHD_{-1} + \theta_{i,11} RHFD_{-1} + \theta_{i,12}$$
$$RCUR_{-1} + \theta_{i,13} RHNFA_{-1} + \theta_{i,14} RHNOA_{-1} \tag{4.4}$$

It should be noted that the θs are the reduced form parameters depending on the structural coefficients of equation **(4.3)** and the adjustment coefficients of equation **(4.2)**. This was demonstrated explicitly in the last chapter.

The consumption function is given by:

$$C = \alpha_0 + \alpha_1 Y + \alpha_2 IFTD(1 - htaxr) + \alpha_3 IFD(1 - htaxr) + \alpha_4 ID(1 - htaxr)$$
$$+ \alpha_5 ITD(1 - htaxr) + \alpha_6 IFO(1 - htaxr) + \alpha_7\pi + \alpha_8 pe + \alpha_9 RHD_{-1}$$
$$+ \alpha_{10} RHFD_{-1} + \alpha_{11} RCUR_{-1} + \alpha_{12} RHNFA_{-1} + \alpha_{13} RHNOA_{-1} \tag{4.5}$$

Note that current wealth is not an argument in the consumption function. This follows from Owen's (1981) assumption that wealth is a consequence of the consumption-savings decision and not a determinant of it.

The final equation we present here is the definition for households' net wealth. This equation is used in the construction of the data set:

$$RHNW = RHD + RHFD + RHNFA + RCUR + RHNOA$$
$$= RHNW_{-1} + RHS \tag{4.6}$$

where RHS is real household saving.

We assume that the own nominal rate of returns has a positive sign in the desired asset demand equations. The signs of the asset returns in the consumption equation are at first unclear on account of conflicting substitution and income effects. Real wealth and real disposable income are assumed to

47

have positive signs in all equations. The lagged assets are assumed to have a positive sign in the consumption equation. We do not impose any symmetry restrictions.

The adding-up restrictions can be derived following the same procedure as in Chapter 3. However, they are somewhat more complicated because of our assumption that the consumption-saving and the portfolio-allocation decisions are integrated rather than sequential. In order to see more clearly the implications of this assumption, it is useful to derive the adding-up restrictions explicitly. However, instead of doing that for the entire model, we follow the procedure of the last chapter and use an illustrative example with two assets, and in this case also the consumption function in its simplified form.

We then assume that the simplified model with only two assets is given as follows:

$$\Delta a_1 = \alpha_{11} Y + \alpha_{12} i_1 + \alpha_{13} i_2 + \alpha_{14} RHNW + \alpha_{15} a_{1_{-1}} + \alpha_{16} a_{2_{-1}} \qquad (4.7)$$

$$\Delta a_2 = \alpha_{21} Y + \alpha_{22} i_1 + \alpha_{23} i_2 + \alpha_{24} RHNW + \alpha_{25} a_{1_{-1}} + \alpha_{26} a_{2_{-1}} \qquad (4.8)$$

$$C = \beta_1 Y + B_2 i_1 + \beta_2 i_2 \qquad (4.9)$$

$$RHNW = RHNW_{-1} + RHS = RHNW_{-1} + Y - C \qquad (4.10)$$

$$Y - C = \Delta a_1 + \Delta a_2 \qquad (4.11)$$

Note that in this simplified model, we have excluded the lagged terms of the assets from the consumption function.

We can easily show that the adding-up restrictions for the above model, in which the portfolio-selection and the consumption-saving decisions are integrated, are given by:

$$[\beta_1(1 - \alpha_{14} - \alpha_{24}) + (\alpha_{11} + \alpha_{14} + \alpha_{21} + \alpha_{24})] = 1$$

$$[\beta_2(1 - \alpha_{14} - \alpha_{24}) + (\alpha_{12} + \alpha_{22})] = 0$$

$$[\beta_3(1 - \alpha_{14} - \alpha_{24}) + (\alpha_{13} + \alpha_{23})] = 0$$

$$(\alpha_{14} + \alpha_{24}) = 0$$

$$(\alpha_{15} + \alpha_{25}) = 0$$

$$(\alpha_{16} + \alpha_{26}) = 0 \qquad (4.12)$$

When the consumption-saving decision is made first and the portfolio-selection decision next, the adding-up restrictions can be derived by setting $\beta_1 = \beta_2 = \beta_3 = 0$. The new restrictions then become:

$$(\alpha_{11} + \alpha_{14} + \alpha_{21} + \alpha_{24}) = 1$$

$$(\alpha_{12} + \alpha_{22}) = 0$$

$$(\alpha_{13} + \alpha_{23}) = 0$$

$$(\alpha_{14} + \alpha_{24}) = 0$$

$$(\alpha_{15} + \alpha_{25}) = 0$$

$$(\alpha_{16} + \alpha_{26}) = 0 \tag{4.13}$$

The model was estimated, first, by imposing the adding-up restrictions in **(4.12)** and then in **(4.13)**.

Estimation results

This section presents the estimation results of the model specified in pp. 44–9. Before presenting the results of this exercise, some explanation of the data used in the estimates is in order. The Appendix to this book gives the entire data set used in the different models. A brief explanation of the construction of some of the main variables used in the estimates will suffice here.

Some variables could be obtained relatively easily. For instance, data with respect to the stock of foreign currency-denominated deposits and zloty deposits held by households, as well as households' demand for currency, have been obtained directly from the NBP information bulletins. The zloty deposit rate and the rate on foreign currency-denominated deposits are proxied by an average of the interest rates on deposits in zlotys and an average of the interest rates on foreign currency-denominated deposits (both given by NBP information bulletins). The inflation rate and the relative change of the exchange rate are proxied by the relative change in the consumer price index and the relative change in the free market exchange rate (also both given by NBP information bulletins). The foreign interest rate has been proxied by the US deposit rate (from IFS reports). Most of the other variables entering the different equations are not directly observable on a monthly basis (or sometimes never), so they have been constructed. The most important variables we had to construct are: households' consumption, households' income, households' demand for foreign assets as well as households' demand for net other assets.

To start with, households' consumption on a monthly basis is approximated by using population figures and quarterly figures on the average monthly per capita expenditures by employees' households (given by Plan-Econ Reports). These figures are adjusted in monthly figures by using the corrected retail sales of goods index, which is also published in the PlanEcon Reports. Households' income has been calculated in line with the specification presented in equation (4.1). Figures on the wage rate and on employment are obtained from the NBP information bulletins, whereas figures on personal (income) taxes are obtained from the PlanEcon reports and figures on government transfers (unemployment benefits etc.) to households are taken from the Statistical Bulletins. As we could not find any information on profit income distributed to households, it is assumed that households receive only labour income. The construction of the stock of net foreign assets held by households is in line with proxies used in the literature to calculate capital flight of a country. The literature gives us several measures to calculate capital flight, depending on what is exactly meant by the term (see e.g., Hermes and Lensink, 1992; Murinde *et al.*, 1996; Lensink *et al.*, 1996). We have used the so-called *residual method*, since this method measures all private capital outflows as being capital flight, and hence provides an estimate of all private capital outflows. This implies that we have proxied the flow demand for net foreign assets by households by the total amount of private capital outflows, and hence implicitly assume that firms do not hold foreign assets. The *residual method* measures capital outflows by comparing the *sources* of capital inflows (net increase of external debt and net inflow of foreign direct investment, both given by NBP PlanEcon Reports) with the *uses* of these inflows (current account deficit and increase in foreign reserves, given by the PlanEcon Reports and the NBP information bulletins, respectively). Finally, the obtained figure has been corrected for the change in net foreign assets held by commercial banks (derived from the NBP bulletins), in order to obtain the change in *private* sector holdings of net foreign assets. Figures on *stocks* of net foreign assets held by households are calculated by summing the lagged stock with the calculated flow figures. The start value for the stock in December 1991 is calculated by using World Bank estimates on flows of capital flight, using the *residual method* (as explained in Claessens and Naudé, 1993), for the 1982–91 period. The stock of capital flight in 1982 is assumed to be zero. Figures on flows of net other assets held by households are calculated by using the budget constraint for households given by equation (4.1), so that a consistent data set is used in the estimates. The stocks of net other assets are calculated by summing the lagged stock with the flow figure. For the first estimation period, the stock of net other assets is assumed to be zero.

In line with the estimation method used for the portfolio model for the commercial banking sector, the model for households has been estimated with the seemingly unrelated regression method. The equation for net other assets is deleted from the system. The model has been estimated by using monthly data on the period December 1991–May 1996.

We can now continue to describe the estimation results. When judging the estimation results it should, however, be taken into account that many variables were not directly available and had to be constructed. As in Chapter 3, we start by presenting the estimation results for the full model (Table 4.2).

Next, Table 4.3 gives the preferred estimation results. Note that we have tried current values of the yield indicators, as well as the one period lagged, two period lagged and one period ahead values. Tables 4.2 and 4.3 give the estimates with the restrictions specified in equation (4.13). We have also estimated the model when the consumption-savings decision and the portfolio decision are sequential. Since the estimates for the sequential model were very similar, they are reported only in the Appendix Table A4.1 (pp. 166–7).

Keeping in mind the data limitations, the results seem quite satisfactory. For purposes of interpretation, we concentrate on the preferred estimates in Table 4.3. We can immediately see that the net worth is not significant in any of the equations, but income is in all but the net foreign assets and foreign currency-denominated time deposits. It also has the correct sign, and it is apparent that the equation giving the least satisfactory result is the one for the net foreign assets. The insignificance of net wealth and the unsatisfactory nature of the equation for the net foreign assets may well have something to do with the possible measurement errors embodied in both variables. But, it is unclear what we can do at this stage. However, the rest of the results, discussed below, suggest that these errors are not fatal enough to render the exercise meaningless.

Turning our attention to the five financial assets, we can see that in each case the own rate of return has the expected sign and is significant. The negative and significant sign of expected inflation in the equation for currency is noteworthy. Similarly, while no symmetry restrictions were imposed, none the less the results (with respect to cross effects of the various rates of return) are not counter-intuitive. These results, in conjunction with the results in Chapter 3 for the commercial banking sector, suggest a prominent role for yields on various assets for the portfolio allocation behaviour of both sectors. The consumption function, while it seems rather simple in the form reported in Table 4.2, is still quite illuminating. A positive and significant coefficient of income and the negative and significant effect of the rate of return on foreign currency-denominated time deposits are noteworthy. Since such deposits still play a prominent role in the Polish household sector portfolio, it is interesting to see that there is yet another channel through which such assets can affect the real side of the economy. Finally, the effects of the various lagged terms in assets are according to predictions and play a significant role in policy simulations reported later on.

Tracking ability of the estimated model

In line with the approach followed in Chapter 3, we test the "fit" of the model by some *ex post* dynamic simulations. We simulate the time path of the real stocks of assets and the change in the real stocks (the flows) of assets, as well as the time path of real consumption. We again use Theil's

Table 4.2 Full model results

	ΔRHFTD	ΔRHFD	ΔRHTD	ΔRHD	ΔRCUR	ΔRHNFA	C
$(1-htaxr)ID$	491011	153301	633224	25628	47974	5333566	-1639924
	(1.24)	(0.76)	(1.92)	(0.22)	(0.09)	(1.20)	(-2.32)
$(1-htaxr)ITD$	-154980	-52438	691262	125851	-610399	-3275091	-258526
	(-0.44)	(-0.29)	(2.38)	(1.23)	(-1.36)	(-0.84)	(-0.39)
$(1-htaxr)IFD$	632123	152426	721290	-735840	3630405	-1708980	52995
	(0.37)	(0.17)	(0.50)	(-1.45)	(1.63)	(-0.09)	(0.02)
$(1-htaxr)IFTD$	-1126180	-501381	266532	225739	-26893	29887007	-8121572
	(-0.70)	(-0.61)	(0.20)	(0.48)	(-0.01)	(1.66)	(-2.95)
$(1-htaxr)IFO$	-2859610	-870625	-3006604	-707675	1028538	-9346949	2641904
	(-2.52)	(-1.56)	(-3.18)	(-2.13)	(0.71)	(-0.74)	(1.25)
pe	24129	11360	-4691.55	129.86	-1387.784	-334659	4229.99
	(3.86)	(3.57)	(-0.90)	(0.07)	(-0.17)	(-4.78)	(0.10)
π	-6888	-2257	-61633.05	-5958.92	-85511	-85736	15427
	(-0.45)	(-0.29)	(-4.84)	(-1.33)	(-4.35)	(-0.50)	(0.53)
Y	0.092	0.119	0.141	0.101	0.237	-1.030	0.739
	(0.87)	(2.22)	(1.61)	(3.28)	(1.76)	(-0.88)	(3.78)
$RHNW$	-0.122	-0.063	0.011	-0.013	0.046	-1.229	
	(-1.42)	(-1.44)	(0.15)	(-0.51)	(0.41)	(-1.27)	

	(1)	(2)	(3)	(4)	(5)	(6)	(7)
$RHFTD_{-1}$	−0.484	−0.101	−0.531	−0.033	0.186	1.851	−0.452
	(−1.73)	(−0.70)	(−2.28)	(−0.41)	(0.52)	(0.59)	(−0.95)
$RHFD_{-1}$	0.624	−0.014	0.597	0.195	−0.247	−3.341	0.066
	(1.74)	(−0.08)	(2.00)	(1.86)	(−0.54)	(−0.83)	(0.10)
$RHTD_{-1}$	−0.122	−0.099	−0.119	0.043	0.086	0.356	−0.226
	(−0.85)	(−1.35)	(−0.99)	(1.01)	(0.46)	(0.22)	(−1.20)
RHD_{-1}	0.027	−0.0005	−0.867	−0.084	0.100	3.857	0.737
	(0.11)	(−0.004)	(−4.64)	(−1.28)	(0.35)	(1.54)	(1.73)
$RCUR_{-1}$	0.113	0.142	−0.023	−0.021	−0.475	0.373	0.388
	(1.13)	(2.80)	(−0.28)	(−0.70)	(−3.70)	(0.33)	(2.40)
$RHNFA_{-1}$	0.075	0.047	−0.010	0.018	−0.011	0.239	0.006
	(0.84)	(1.04)	(−0.13)	(0.68)	(−0.09)	(0.24)	(0.12)
$RHNOA_{-1}$	0.113	0.066	0.021	0.017	−0.042	0.837	−0.021
	(1.27)	(1.45)	(0.28)	(0.65)	(−0.36)	(0.84)	(−0.70)
Constant	56314	17168	2612.73	−7082	−4798	511840	39120
	(2.53)	(1.52)	(0.14)	(−1.09)	(−0.17)	(2.06)	(0.93)
Obs.	53	53	53	53	53	53	53
adj. R^2	0.51	0.51	0.75	0.51	0.52	0.47	0.37
DW	2.63	1.52	1.81	2.43	2.12	2.18	1.49

Table 4.3 Preferred model results

	$\Delta RHFTD$	$\Delta RHFD$	$\Delta RHTD$	ΔRHD	$\Delta RCUR$	$\Delta RHNFA$	C
$(1-htaxr_{-1})ID_{-1}$				183717 (2.75)			-3707762 (-5.22)
$(1-htaxr)ITD$		-154740 (-2.60)	606183 (5.38)				
$(1-htaxr)IFD$		1104779 (2.28)					
$(1-htaxr)IFTD$	320556 (1.80)	-782040 (-3.64)					
$(1-htaxr)IFO$	-400895 (-3.23)			-437190 (-4.34)			
pe	27674 (5.35)	16579 (6.45)					
π			-64657 (-6.14)		-74662 (-5.41)		
Y		0.133 (4.97)	0.127 (1.78)	0.092 (5.33)	0.242 (3.40)		
$RHNW$							0.582 (5.58)
$RHFTD_{-1}$			-0.144 (-6.36)	-0.014 (-2.26)			

$RHFD_{-1}$			−0.159 (−2.22)			−0.051 (−2.46)	−0.034 (−4.32)
$RHTD_{-1}$		0.573 (2.49)			−0.053 (−2.61)		
RHD_{-1}							
$RCUR_{-1}$			−0.302 (−4.35)	−0.059 (−5.08)			
$RHNFA_{-1}$	0.244 (3.42)	−0.975 (−5.24)	0.038 (2.52)		−0.024 (−7.80)		
$RHNOA_{-1}$	0.019 (5.56)	−0.482 (−5.09)	0.020 (2.51)	0.002 (6.72)			
Constant		268257 (4.85)					
Obs.	53	53	53	52	53	53	53
R^2	0.38	0.29	0.60	0.57	0.70	0.45	0.47
SD DEPV	2520.47	16145.20	1934.55	437.82	1835.71	762.18	1502.22
SQ RES	2.04E+08	9.57E+09	78635044	4189482	53279644	16509492	61917880
MEAN DV	36451.17	−8424.23	42.11	294.08	1092.93	42.27	−10.63
SE Reg	2039.322	13973.18	1293.478	301.7875	1064.711	599.0843	1129.815
DW	1.12	1.84	2.03	2.12	1.06	1.59	2.22

inequality coefficient, the coefficient of determination (R^2) and the mean error of the forecasts as test variables. In these simulations, as well as the simulations in the next section, real disposable income of households, the tax rate, the rate of inflation, the expected relative change in the exchange rate as well as the different nominal interest rates are treated as exogenous variables. In the simulations with the full model (see Chapter 7), most of these variables become endogenous.

The figures below present simulated and actual behaviour of consumption (Figure 4.5); the stock of currency (Figure 4.6); the stock of zloty demand deposits (Figure 4.7); the stock of foreign currency-denominated demand deposits (Figure 4.8); the stock of foreign currency-denominated time deposits (Figure 4.9); the stock of net other assets (Figure 4.10); the stock of zloty time deposits (Figure 4.11) and the stock of net foreign assets (Figure 4.12).

The results in Table 4.4 can be read like the corresponding results in Chapter 3; the figures are more illuminating for our purpose. As was implied by the estimates in Tables 4.2 and 4.3, the consumption equation gives the least satisfactory results in terms of the model's ability to track the time path. This poor result is more marked for the period after mid-1995. A more detailed analysis of this equation may reveal the underlying causes, but such an exercise is beyond the scope of the present study. The simulated and the actual values of the five financial assets seem to follow reasonably closely, at least as far as the direction of changes is concerned. In terms of the quantitative closeness of the two series, we do notice some differences. In some cases, the model over-predicts, while in the others, it under-predicts. However, it seems that the tracking ability of the model for the most recent period is not

Table 4.4 Test results: dynamic simulations

	R^2	TC
$\Delta RHNOA$	undef	0.913
$\Delta RHFD$	0.382	0.511
$\Delta RHFTD$	0.471	0.607
ΔRHD	0.542	0.546
$\Delta RHTD$	0.609	0.405
$\Delta RCUR$	0.420	0.513
$\Delta RHNFA$	0.076	0.886
C	0.273	0.490
$RHNOA$	0.995	0.405
$RHFTD$	0.453	0.503
$RHTD$	0.864	0.286
$RCUR$	0.672	0.466
$RHNFA$	0.982	0.616
$RHFD$	0.652	0.464
RHD	0.911	0.306

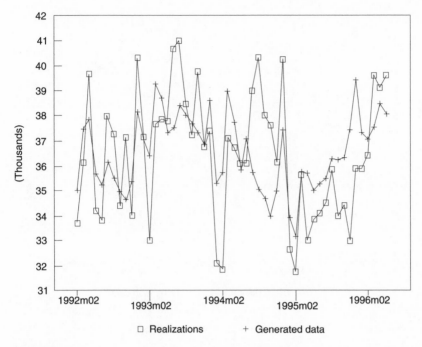

Figure 4.5 C

as good as that for the earlier period. It would be interesting to examine this aspect of our results in greater detail.

Illustrative policy simulations

This section presents some illustrative policy simulations. As in Chapter 3, we start with a base simulation in which all exogenous variables (*ID*, *ITD*, *IFD*, *IFTD*, *IFO*, *htaxr*, *pe*, *Y*, and π) are set at their May 1996 (see Appendix to the book) value during the whole simulation period and subsequently simulate the model by changing the value of one of the exogenous variables. The policy simulations refer to changes in the four nominal interest rates (*ID*, *ITD*, *IFD*, *IFTD*), which are under control of the Polish government. For all cases we have assessed the effect of a 25 per cent increase. The figures show the deviations from the base run. The first simulation refers to an increase in the demand deposit rate on foreign currency-denominated demand deposits. Figures 4.13 (p. 61) and 4.14 (p. 62) present the results of this simulation. The figures do not need more explanation. The behaviour of the different stocks of assets is, in general, in line with expectations. The demand for foreign currency-denominated demand deposits increases, whereas the demand for zloty time deposits, currency and net other assets goes down. It

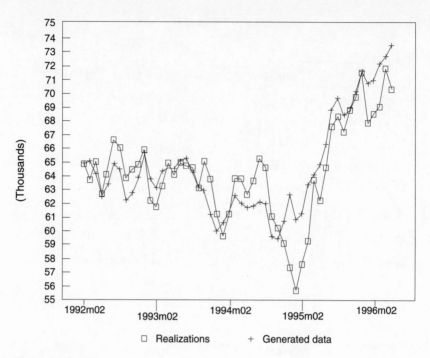

Figure 4.6 RCUR

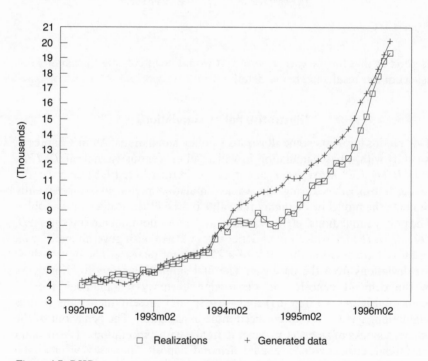

Figure 4.7 RHD

58

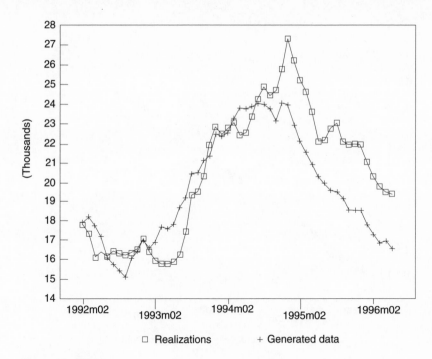

Figure 4.8 RHFD

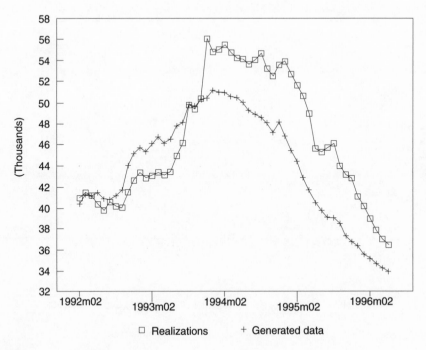

Figure 4.9 RHFTD

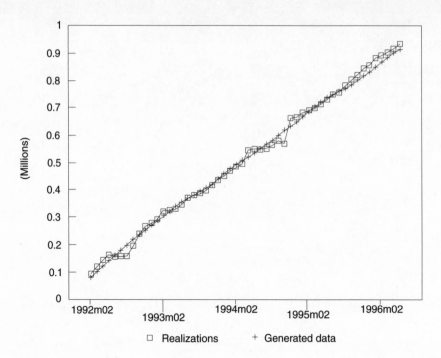

Figure 4.10   RHNOA

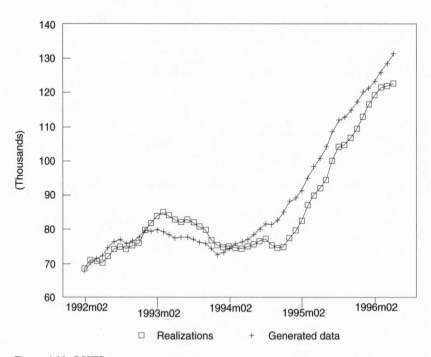

Figure 4.11   RHTD

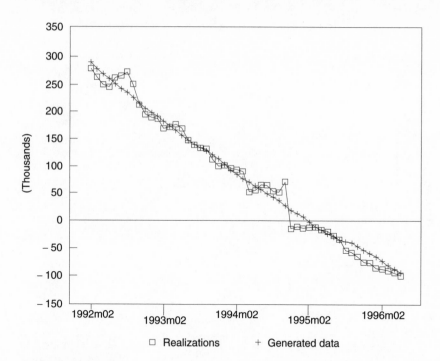

Figure 4.12 *RHNFA*

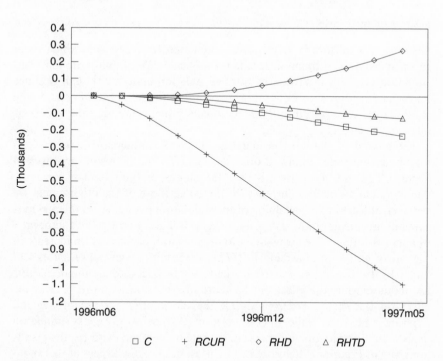

Figure 4.13 Increase in *IFD*

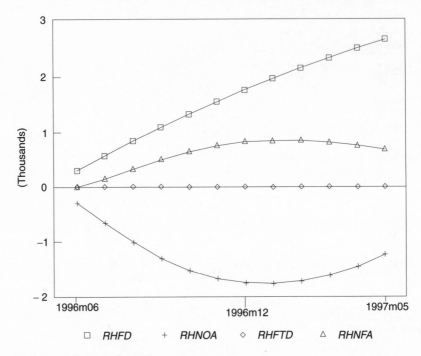

Figure 4.14 Increase in *IFD*

has no effect on foreign currency-denominated time deposits, which is no surprise given the estimation results for this asset. We should note that consumption goes down during the whole simulation period, although *IFD* has no direct effect on consumption. This confirms the relevance of considering feedback effects, and not only direct effects, when examining the effects of interest rate changes.

The second simulation considers the effects of an increase in the rate on foreign currency-denominated time deposits (*IFTD*); the results are given in Figures 4.15 and 4.16. In this case the shares of both foreign currency-denominated assets and currency go up, while those of the other assets are reduced, at least in the beginning of the simulation period. As in the previous simulation, consumption also goes down, although its time path is somewhat different this time. The next simulation relates to the effects of an increase in the rate of return on time deposits (*ITD*); the results are given in Figures 4.17 and 4.18. In this case the shares of the foreign-currency denominated assets are reduced while the effect on the share of own asset is positive, as is the effect on the share of currency. But the effect on the share of demand deposits is negative, while on consumption it is positive. The last simulation deals with the effect of an increase in the rate on demand deposits; the results are given in Figures 4.19 and 4.20. The most noteworthy aspect of this simulation is that it produces the opposite results to that of the previous one in

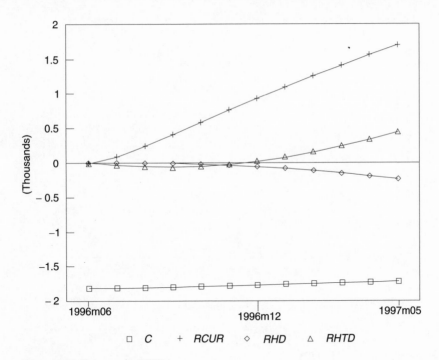

Figure 4.15 Increase in *IFTD*

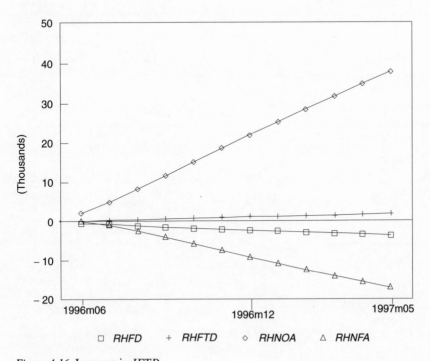

Figure 4.16 Increase in *IFTD*

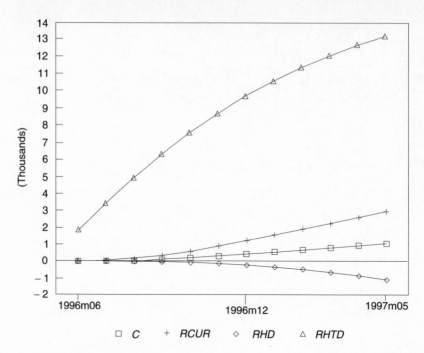

Figure 4.17 Increase in *ITD*

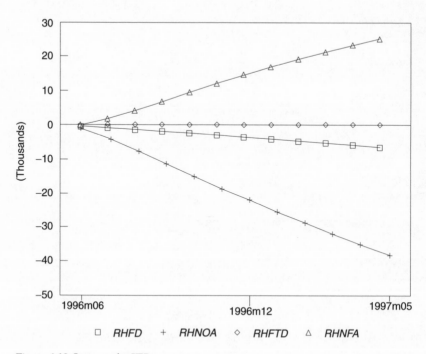

Figure 4.18 Increase in *ITD*

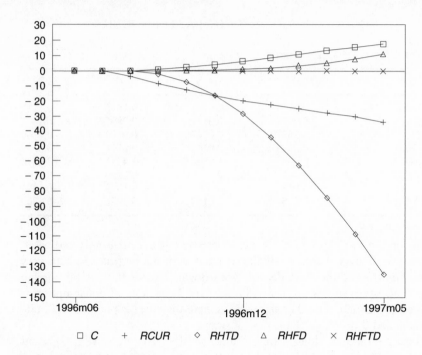

Figure 4.19 Increase in *ID*

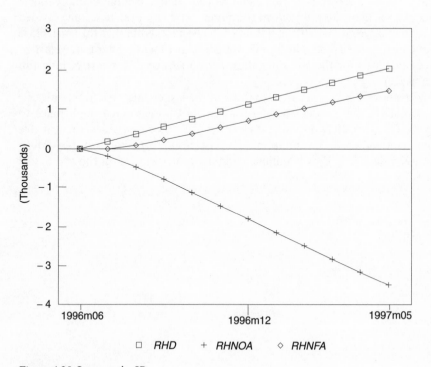

Figure 4.20 Increase in *ID*

Table 4.5 Interest rate elasticities

Increase	IDD	IFD	IFTD	ITD
C	0.0019	−0.0241	−0.1816	0.1112
RCUR	−0.0017	−0.0551	0.0865	0.1472
RHD	0.2659	0.0347	−0.0287	−0.1381
RHTD	−0.0033	−0.0142	0.0111	0.3239
RHFD	0.0045	1.0806	−1.4215	−2.6578
RHFTD	0	0	0.2296	0
RHNOA	−0.013	−0.0045	0.1375	−0.1391
RHNFA	−0.035	−0.0153	0.3971	−0.5803

terms of the responses of the other domestic currency-denominated asset. Thus, in this case the share of the demand deposits increases, albeit, very little, but that of the time deposit goes down. Except that of the foreign assets, all other shares go down. Finally, the behaviour of consumption is interesting. Unlike the other simulations, here the effect is positive and quite pronounced throughout the period of simulation.

Note that the above figures are not dimensionless. Therefore, we also present a table (Table 4.5) in which the effect of the increase in the rates is given as an elasticity. The elasticity is calculated as the relative change of the variable under consideration (alternative run minus base run over base run) divided by the relative change of the relevant interest rate. Note that this variable is not constant over time. The figures presented in Table 4.5 refer to the elasticities calculated for the last simulation period (hence it is a sort of long-run elasticity).

The above simulations are, like those in the last chapter, based on only one block of the full model, therefore, we do not attach much importance to them. However, they do make it clear that this block provides a reasonable characterization of consumption and portfolio behaviour of the Polish households and is thus a suitable candidate for inclusion in the full model later on.

5

THE FIRM

In this chapter we turn to the behaviour of the firm in the Polish economy. The analysis of this sector poses some serious problems. This is because the Polish economy is characterized by a sizeable state enterprise sector so that we really have two types of firms – private and state enterprises or public firms. Ideally, therefore, the correct way to proceed would be to specify a two-sub-sector model where these two types of firms are distinguished separately. Unfortunately this approach is not feasible due to lack of data. For example, starting with the basic variable, which is the main objective of this chapter, namely, investment expenditure, while the data are available for a short period of time, the actual meaning of the breakdown is suspect. This is due to the process of privatization. The process itself sometimes ends up classifying certain investments as belonging to the private sector rather than as actually having taken place there. Therefore, it is questionable whether for purposes of analysis this kind of distinction can be taken seriously. Apart from this, there are also problems with other data. Here are just a few examples. The data on bank loans refer to all loans to this sector rather than to the public and the private sector. Similarly, the data on the holdings of various financial assets – zloty demand and time deposits and foreign currency demand and time deposits – are given as holdings by the two types of firms together. The same also holds true of the various rates of return as well as loan rates and the rate of profitability. These data shortcomings and the problems in definition compel us to treat the two types of firms as if they were identical in their behaviour. This is clearly unsatisfactory because of its behavioural implications. At this point obviously nothing can be done. Hopefully, when appropriate data become available, it would be useful to proceed by disaggregating this sector. In the meantime, in the next section we will discuss the relative importance of these two types of firms.

Some statistical background

We start with Figure 5.1, which gives the monthly behaviour of total, private and public investments. The close correspondence between all three is

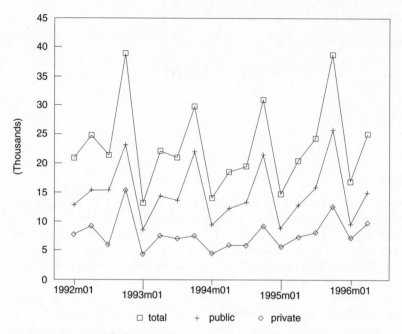

Figure 5.1 Real investments

obvious. But it does not show the relative importance of the two types of firms in total investment. This aspect is shown in Figure 5.2. It is clear from this figure that there is considerable variability in the share of private investment. For example, the share ranges from a low of about 28 per cent in mid-1993 to a high of almost 43 per cent in early 1996, thus suggesting a difference of almost 15 per cent. It is thus clear that the relative share of private investment varies enough to demand an explanation. But, it is also clear, as mentioned above, that some of this difference may purely be the result of classification as a consequence of privatization. Be that as it may, it is clear that since the relative role of the public enterprises is likely to diminish as time goes by, it will make sense to distinguish between the two types of firms if and when the relevant data become available.

Since the primary aim of this chapter is to examine the behaviour of investment, we next consider how it varied in response to some of the determinants. We again follow the same approach as in Chapters 3 and 4, that is, we look at the regularities between the behaviour of investment and some of its determinants. These regularities, or lack therein, are not meant to suggest either causalities or firm confirmation of any hypotheses, but merely as suggestions of possibilities. To this end, we first consider Figure 5.3. This figure shows the behaviour of aggregate bank loans to the firms – both public

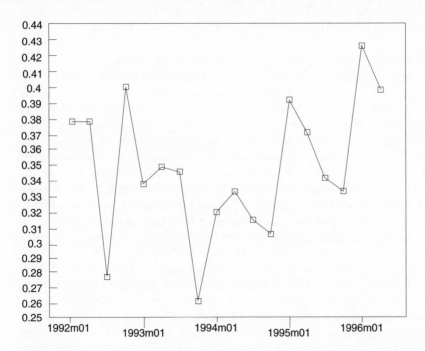

Figure 5.2 Share of private investment

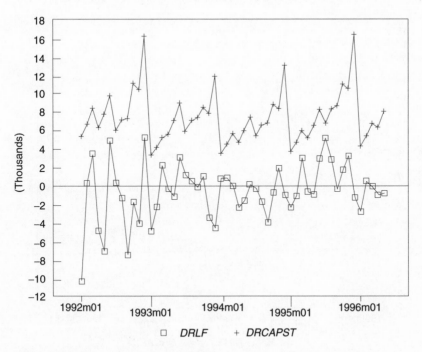

Figure 5.3 Real investment and bank loans

and private together – and total investment. Except for the period towards the end, the positive correspondence between the two variables is quite suggestive. This may not be surprising since investment depends to some extent on the availability of investible funds, quite apart from its cost. The next variable we consider is the profit rate. The profit rate is not what we would ideally like it to be, but it is the rate of return on turnover as given in NBP bulletins. This measures the profit rate on total turnover. Furthermore, it is not clear whether the coverage of the firms for this variable and for the calculation of investment is identical. In any event, this is the only measure of profitability we have available at this time. Keeping this in mind, Figure 5.4 plots the two variables. It is evident that there was not much variability in the rate of profit during the period covered, but there is still suggested some positive correspondence between investment and the profit rate.

Next, we look at the relationship with three other variables: retained earnings, bank loan rate and direct foreign investment. The relationship between retained earnings and investment is shown in Figure 5.5. On the whole a positive relationship is discernible, although some points of a negative relationship can also be seen, particularly at the beginning of the period. This relationship indicates the importance of internal funds for investment decisions and accords well with the existing empirical literature on this subject. The effect of the cost of loanable funds is shown in Figure 5.6. The cost

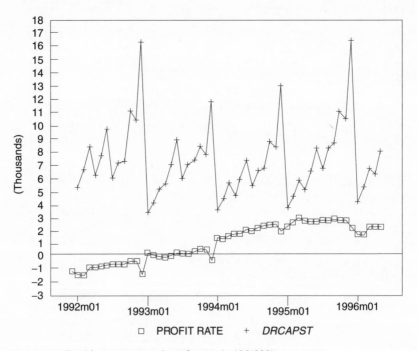

Figure 5.4 Real investment and profit rate ($\times$ 100,000)

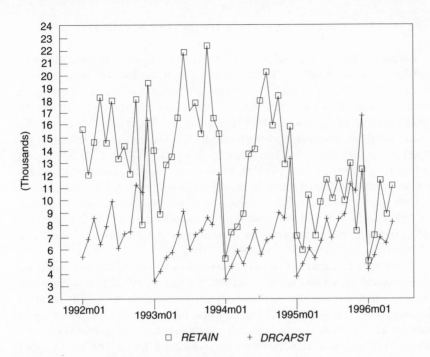

Figure 5.5 Investment and retained earnings

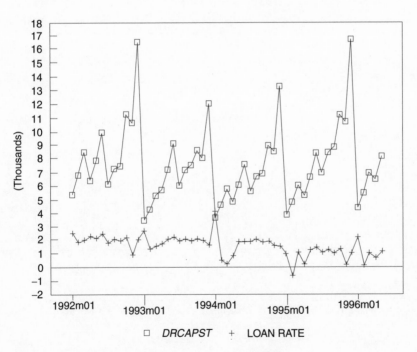

Figure 5.6 Investment and bank loan rate (× 1,000,000)

here is represented by the real-after-tax loan rate. The expected negative relationship is not so evident. When viewed against the role of bank loans in Figure 5.3, this could indicate that investment decisions in Poland are much more constrained by the availability of funds than by their cost. Finally, the effect of direct foreign investment is graphed in Figure 5.7. Assuming that direct foreign investment represents another source of loanable funds, the expected positive relationship is not surprising, although it does not appear to be strong. As mentioned before, these diagrammatic representations are not necessarily any indications of causal relationships or their strengths, but they do seem to indicate that variables which are commonly used to explain the behaviour of investment expenditure may also have a role in explaining such expenditures in Poland. The rationale for the inclusion of these and other variables is explained in the next section.

Since we are going to follow the same strategy for modelling the behaviour of investment as we did in the chapters for the households and the commercial banks, namely, the portfolio selection approach, we briefly mention the other assets considered. The asset menu in this sector consists of, apart from investment, four types of deposits: zloty demand and time deposits and foreign currency-denominated demand and time deposits and finally other assets. Given the difficulties of measuring capital stock, we do not show the

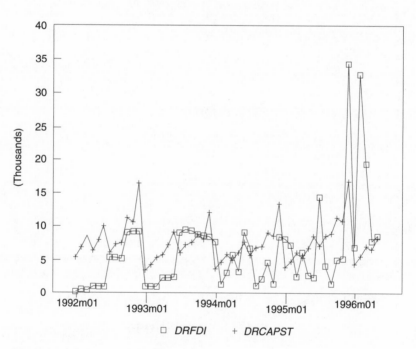

Figure 5.7 Investment and foreign direct investment (× 10)

relative sizes of these various assets. But in the next section, we explain the behaviour of all of the assets considered in this chapter.

What is clear from the brief discussion above is that there have been considerable variations in the behaviour of total investment as well as in the shares of public and private investments over the period covered in this study. In addition, casual observation of the data suggests that some of the more common determinants of investment would seem to be relevant in the determination of the behaviour of investment in Poland. Whether and the extent to which they are indeed significant is the question examined in the next two sections.

The model

The derivation of the model for firms is very much like the model for the household sector. Basically, it is a Tobin-like portfolio model in which the capital stock is seen as one of the assets of the portfolio of firms. Hence, we use a model in which the investment equation, and the other asset demand equations, are derived from a portfolio framework. Since the model is well known, and since the main issues of the model are explained in Chapters 2 and 3, we can be brief here. The real budget constraint for firms reads as:

$$RETAIN = \Delta RCD + \Delta RCTD + \Delta RCFD + \Delta RCFTD + \Delta RCAPST +$$

$$\Delta RCNOA - \Delta RL_f - \Delta RFDI \tag{5.1}$$

where RCD = real stock of zloty demand deposits; $RCTD$ = real stock of zloty time deposits; $RCFD$ = real stock of foreign currency demand deposits held at Polish commercial banks; $RCFTD$ = real stock of foreign currency time deposits held at Polish commercial banks; the C in the beginning of those variables denotes "held by the corporate sector"; $RETAIN$ denotes retained earnings; $\Delta RCAPST$ denotes real gross investment; RL_f denotes real stock of bank loans for firms; $\Delta RFDI$ is the flow of real foreign direct investment and $RCNOA$ is the net other assets held by the corporate sector. Δ = a change in a variable.

The above equation shows that firms finance their demand for different assets by retained earnings, domestic bank loans and foreign direct investments.

In line with the last two chapters asset demands are derived from a multi-variable adjustment process. We have assumed that firms are credit-constrained, and hence take all of the domestic bank loans and foreign direct investments they can get. This implies that firms' portfolio model consists of six asset demand equations: for $\Delta RCAPST$; ΔRCD; $\Delta RCTD$; $\Delta RCFD$; $\Delta RCFTD$ and $\Delta RCNOA$. Taking into account yield rates on all of the different assets and the fact that we assume that firms are credit-constrained, a "typical" asset demand equation looks like:

$$\Delta ac_i = \eta_{i,0}RETAIN + \eta_{i,2}ID(1 - ctaxr) + \eta_{i,3}IFD(1 - ctaxr) +$$
$$\eta_{i,4}IFTD(1 - ctaxr) + \eta_{i,5}ITD(1 - ctaxr) + \eta_{i,6}\pi +$$
$$\eta_{i,7}IK(1 - ctaxr) + \eta_{i,8}IF(1 - ctaxr) + \eta_{i,9}pe +$$
$$\eta_{1,10}\Delta RL_f + \eta_{i,11}RFDI + \eta_{i,12}RCAPST_{-1} + \eta_{i,13}RCFTD_{-1} +$$
$$\eta_{i,14}RCFD_{-1} + \eta_{i,15}RCNOA_{-1} + \eta_{i,16}RCTD_{-1} + \eta_{i,17}RCD_{-1} + \eta_{i,18}$$

$$(5.2)$$

where ID is the zloty demand deposit rate; IFD the foreign currency demand deposit rate; ITD the zloty time deposit rate; $IFTD$ the foreign currency time deposit rate; IF the bank loan rate for firms; IK a proxy for the return on capital; pe the expected relative change in the exchange rate; $ctaxr$ is the corporate tax rate.

The typical asset equation for this sector needs some explanation, first concerning the inclusion of retained earnings, which follows from the budget constraint. Its economic rationale is clear from the literature in that firms more often than not depend on internal funds for their financial needs. The inclusion of loans and direct foreign investment may seem like double counting, but our argument is that these items from the liabilities side shed important light on the behaviour of firms as far as their investment decisions are concerned. Both constitute borrowed sources of funds and to the extent that firms are assumed to be credit constrained it is important to assess the significance of this assumption. The inclusion of these variables may also shed some light on the relative importance of financing investment from domestic and foreign funds. The inclusion of the cost of bank loans is meant to capture the basic idea that not only the availability but also the cost of domestic funds may be relevant. This channel may well work through the profitability of the firms. The inclusion of the various rates of return, including the expected relative change in the exchange rate, follows from the standard theory of portfolio selection.

In the actual estimates we face quite a few problems of measurement. Beginning with the main one – that is, capital stock – we could not find any initial stock of capital, so we had to approximate it by an admittedly arbitrary procedure, which assumed that it was three times the real GDP in 1991. This could introduce measurement error of unknown magnitude. The rates of returns and the loan rate are net of taxes and they are nominal. There are obviously two ways of introducing inflation. One is to calculate all rates of return in real terms and the other is to use inflation as a separate variable and to use nominal rates net of taxes. The choice depends on how one views the reaction of firms to inflation. We take the same view we have in the chapters on households and the commercial banks and therefore introduced inflation as a separate variable. However, we did estimate the model also by using real rates and the difference was not significant. The difficulties with the profit rate used have already been explained above.

Estimation results

We start by presenting the OLS estimates per equation for the "full model". Table 5.1 gives the results. Next, we reestimate the model by first deleting variables with very low t-value (except for the own rate of return). After

Table 5.1 The results for the full model*

	$\Delta RCAPS$	ΔRCD	$\Delta RCTD$	$\Delta RCFTD$	$\Delta RCFD$
RETAIN	0.288	0.065	0.078	0.0049	0.0081
	(2.51)	(0.42)	(1.82)	(0.37)	(0.52)
$(1-ctaxr)ID$	−110523	1437048	−166809	−120966	158553
	(−0.15)	(1.42)	(−0.59)	(−1.37)	(1.55)
$(1-ctaxr)IFD$	−3256342	−1208215	3746977	211537	−913188
	(−1.11)	(−0.31)	(3.42)	(0.62)	(−2.29)
$(1-ctaxr)IFTD$	3831850	−19812	306329	−192949	108554
	(1.96)	(−0.01)	(0.41)	(−0.85)	(0.41)
$(1-ctaxr)ITD$	1108712	1589083	−417053	−97541	266429
	(1.86)	(1.99)	(−1.87)	(−1.40)	(3.28)
π	−10705	−205588	−9006	−4600	−6802.6
	(−0.24)	(−3.51)	(−0.55)	(−0.90)	(−1.14)
$(1-ctaxr)IK$	−416661	−884798	169378	6367.7	−23827
	(−3.13)	(−4.98)	(3.41)	(0.41)	(−1.32)
$(1-ctaxr)IF$	−1107360	−959522	−84239	80485	−172153
	(−2.59)	(−1.68)	(−0.53)	(1.62)	(−2.97)
pe	7354.71	−21604	−4252.56	1051.69	837.08
	(0.73)	(−1.60)	(−1.12)	(0.89)	(0.61)
ΔRL_f	0.142	−0.3774	0.0463	−0.0089	−0.041
	(0.94)	(−1.87)	(0.82)	(−0.50)	(−1.98)
$\Delta RFDI$	0.212	−0.4799	0.3991	0.0170	0.1495
	(0.36)	(−0.60)	(1.79)	(0.24)	(1.85)
$RCAPST_{-1}$	0.0185	−0.0288	−0.0078	−0.0029	0.012
	(0.66)	(−0.77)	(−0.75)	(−0.90)	(3.15)
$RCFTD_{-1}$	0.1665	0.6230	0.1787	−0.2419	0.055
	(0.18)	(0.49)	(0.51)	(−2.20)	(0.43)
$RCFD_{-1}$	−3.3715	−2.9915	0.5264	0.2196	−0.5562
	(−3.78)	(−2.51)	(1.58)	(2.11)	(−4.59)
$RCNOA_{-1}$	0.0364	0.1311	−0.0102	0.0029	−0.0093
	(1.21)	(3.26)	(−0.91)	(0.83)	(−2.26)
$RCTD_{-1}$	0.1055	0.3894	−0.3314	−0.0024	−0.0314
	(0.40)	(1.11)	(−3.37)	(−0.08)	(−0.88)
RCD_{-1}	0.019	−0.5207	0.0273	0.0166	−0.0072
	(0.15)	(−3.17)	(0.60)	(1.16)	(−0.43)
Constant	−39020	53264	27696.7	6237.6	−23267
	(−0.74)	(0.76)	(1.41)	(1.02)	(−3.26)
Obs.	53	53	53	53	53
adj. R^2	0.63	0.65	0.53	0.14	0.46
DW	1.41	2.02	2.59	1.98	2.07

* "t" values are given in parentheses.

some reestimations we select preferred specifications. The Zellner estimates for the preferred specifications are given in Table 5.2.

Although our main discussion of the results will be based on the preferred estimates, a word is in order on the results of the full model. We consider the signs and the significance of the three main variables of interest, namely, retained earnings, bank loans and the loan rate. Considering the equation of the main concern in this chapter, that is for investment, we can see that all three variables have the expected sign, while the degree of their significance is somewhat different. The overall "fit" of the equation is satisfactory, particularly given the fact that equations for investment are notoriously difficult to fit.

We now concentrate on the preferred estimates in Table 5.2. Here the results are far more suggestive. Retained earnings are now highly significant with a positive sign, and they seem to affect investment in physical capital only, thus suggesting that all retained earnings are used for this purpose, and for net other assets, only. Similarly, the coefficient of the loan rate now becomes highly significant with the expected negative sign. The positive sign of inflation may seem counterintuitive, but in fact it is not. The positive sign simply means that with the nominal after-tax rate on bank loans remaining constant, an increase in inflation implies a reduction in the real rate and hence an increase in investment, thus implying a positive coefficient of inflation. The significance of this coefficient when noted along with the significance of the nominal loan rate is particularly important, because it implies that a reduction in the real loan rate, whether brought about by inflation or by changes in the nominal rate has the desired effect on investment activities. But, at the same time, the quantitative effects of the two modes are not the same, which confirms the advisability of treating inflation and the nominal rates as separate arguments as we have done. Equally interesting is the positive and the significant effect of bank loans. This confirms our hypothesis that both the quantity and the cost of bank loans are important determinants of investment in Poland. This means that even though the Polish firms are assumed to be liquidity constrained and will take all the loans that they can get, they do take the cost of such loans seriously, presumably with the mechanism being from the profit side. The role of foreign direct investment is also confirmed. Finally, there are the coefficients of the lagged and the other rates of returns. As shown in Chapters 3 and 4, with their coefficients being combinations of various structural parameters, it is difficult to offer a straightforward rationalization.

Turning to the estimates for the other equations, we concentrate on the signs and the significance of the own rates of returns. It can be easily seen that they have the correct sign in the respective equations. Note that with respect to the equation for $\Delta RCFTD$ the own rate of return is reflected by the expected rate of depreciation. Although the own rate of return in the

Table 5.2 The results for preferred specifications*

	$\Delta RCAPST$	ΔRCD	$\Delta RCTD$	$\Delta RCFTD$	$\Delta RCFD$
RETAIN	0.3595 (6.27)				
$(1-ctaxr)ID$		1169369 (2.39)			
$(1-ctaxr)IFD$					58317 (0.79)
$(1-ctaxr)IFTD$	3884188 (6.05)				
$(1-ctaxr)ITD$		523956 (2.75)	308122 (3.97)	−75683 (−3.18)	
π	65939 (2.42)	−95412 (−3.98)	−29047 (−3.56)		
$(1-ctaxr)IK$		−601268 (−7.33)			
$(1-ctaxr)IF$	−674631 (−6.15)		−249348 (−3.27)	64706 (3.09)	
pe				2173 (2.53)	
ΔRL_f	0.3706 (3.48)				
$\Delta RFDI$	1.2090 (3.56)				0.2304 (4.42)
$RCAPST_{-1}$	0.0037 (5.38)	−0.060 (−3.19)			
$RCFTD_{-1}$				−0.0920 (−2.52)	−0.1053 (1.43)
$RCFD_{-1}$	−2.069 (−4.94)	−0.9366 (−1.68)		0.1094 (3.09)	−0.1340 (−2.44)
$RCNOA_{-1}$		0.1362 (6.09)			0.0012 (1.88)
$RCTD_{-1}$		0.5773 (3.89)	−0.1597 (−3.52)		
RCD_{-1}		−0.5944 (−6.77)			
Constant		111007 (3.01)	5675 (3.03)		
Obs.	53	53	53	53	53
R^2	0.64	0.70	0.40	0.23	0.35
SD DEPV	2820.194	3895.501	939.2935	216.2877	316.3647
SQ RES	1.50E+08	2.33E+08	27564370	1872273	3379559
MEAN DV	7540.158	−242.2648	162.1948	34.48785	25.85700
SE Reg	1826.768	2329.351	757.7979	197.4986	265.3441
DW	1.37	2.16	1.78	1.79	1.93

* "t" values are given in parentheses.

equation for $\Delta RCFD$ is not striking at the usual significance levels, for theoretical reasons we have decided to take it into account in the simulations. As for the cross-effects, since we have not imposed the restriction of symmetry, it is not possible to say much about their signs.

What can we conclude from the above discussion? The main conclusion would seem to be that given the shortcomings of the data, particularly with respect to our inability to estimate separate functions for private and public firms, the estimates for investment are quite satisfactory in that they, at least, suggest expected outcome with respect to the influence of main determinants. The results are particularly revealing in terms of the role that variables of concern play in this study, namely, the financial variables. In our case, they are the bank loans and their cost. It is also revealing that the rates of return on other assets held by the firms may have consequences for investment decisions. This aspect is not often recognized in studies of investment behaviour, but this may be particularly crucial for transition economies where the process of financial deregulation affects the whole structure of interest rates and not just selected ones. The importance of this feature will be examined in the simulations later on in this chapter as well in the simulations of the full model in later chapters.

Tracking ability of the estimated model

Following the procedure in the last two chapters, here also we examine the tracking ability of the estimated model. We do this, as before, by carrying out *ex post* dynamic simulations. The simulations are carried out by using the preferred estimates in Table 5.2.

For reasons of space we will not present all of the figures. As in Chapter 3 we present the results for the real "stocks" only. However, since we are mainly interested in the tracking ability of our model with respect to real investments, we also present the real investments (change in the stock of capital). The results are given in Figures 5.8–5.14.

Given our main interest in this chapter, we first consider Figures 5.8 and 5.9. Figure 5.8 plots the actual and the forecasted values of real investment, while Figure 5.9 does the same for real capital stock. In both cases the model seems to do a reasonable job of tracking. As we know from the previous chapters, since the values of the stocks are endogenously determined in dynamic simulations, such tracking is even more remarkable. Perhaps a rather nice test of the tracking ability of the model is to look at the outcome with respect to "net other assets", which is the residual category. From Figure 5.14 we can see that the actual and the predicted values move reasonably together, in particular during the more recent period.

As before, we can also examine the tracking ability by looking at the various statistics about the actual and the forecasted values. The relevant information is given in Table 5.3. If we look at the Theil Coefficient (TC), we

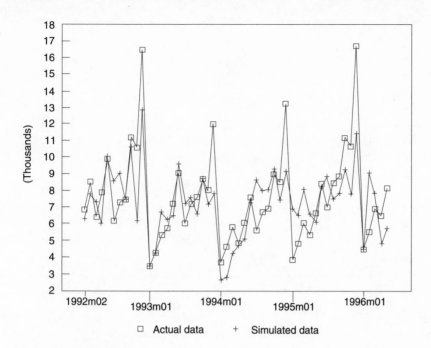

Figure 5.8 DRCAPST

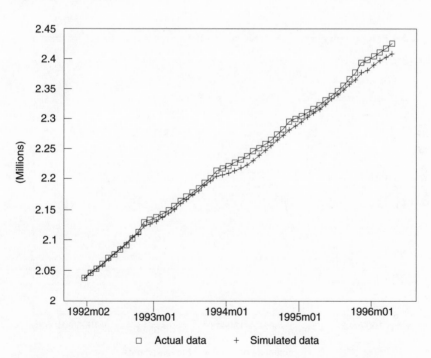

Figure 5.9 RCAPST

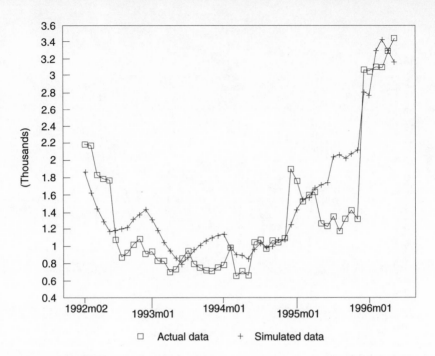

Figure 5.10 RCFD

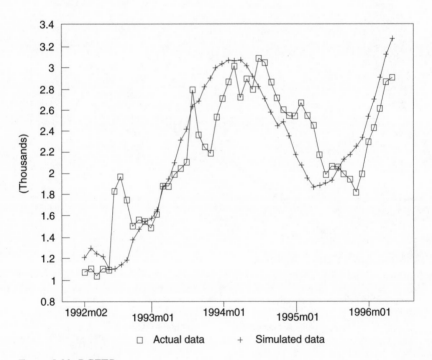

Figure 5.11 RCFTD

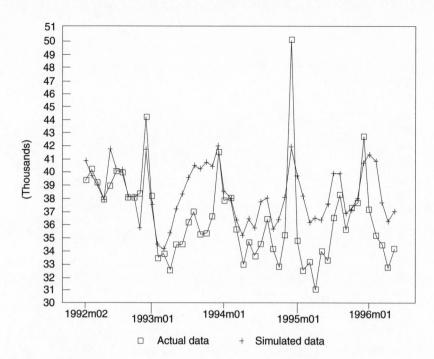

Figure 5.12 RCD

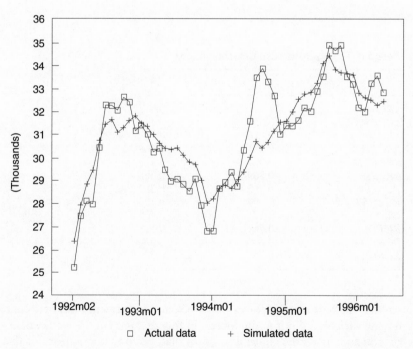

Figure 5.13 RCTD

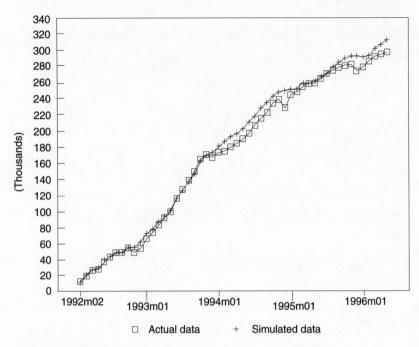

Figure 5.14 RCNOA

Table 5.3 Test results for dynamic simulations

	R^2	TC
$\Delta RCNOA$	0.418	0.577
$\Delta RCAPST$	0.524	0.342
ΔRCD	0.416	0.54
$\Delta RCTD$	0.331	0.668
$\Delta RCFTD$	0.052	0.716
$\Delta RCFD$	0.269	0.586
$RCNOA$	0.992	0.282
$RCAPST$	0.993	0.125
RCD	0.174	0.509
$RCTD$	0.761	0.518
$RCFTD$	0.649	0.628
$RCFD$	0.757	0.562

can see that the best result is for capital stock and investment (and net other assets), the variables of our main interest in this chapter. On the whole, then, we can conclude from the above discussion that, given the limitations of the data, the results presented above are satisfactory as at least a starting point.

Partial and selected policy simulations

While more accurate implications of the various interest rate deregulation policies can only be carried out with the full model, like Chapters 3 and 4, it is still worthwhile having a first look at some of the effects in a partial framework. Therefore, in this section we examine the effects of changes in the loan rate, the supply of bank loans and the interest rate on zloty time deposits. Each one of these variables would highlight different aspects of financial deregulation.

The procedure for the simulations is as follows. We start with a base simulation in which the values for *ID*, *IFD*, *IFTD*, *ITD*, *IK*, *IH*, *pe* and π are assumed to be equal to the June 1996 value during the whole simulation period. The other exogenous variables, i.e., ΔRL_f, $\Delta RFDI$, *ctaxr*, and *RETAIN* are assumed to be equal to their average value during the estimation period. In the alternative simulation we assume an increase of 25 per cent of one of the exogenous variables. The figures show the difference between the outcomes in the alternative run and the base run, and hence show the effects of the shock. Results for the different stocks in the portfolio of the firms are shown.

We consider the effect of an increase in bank loans. This is shown in Figures 5.15 (for effects on net other assets, capital stock and zloty demand

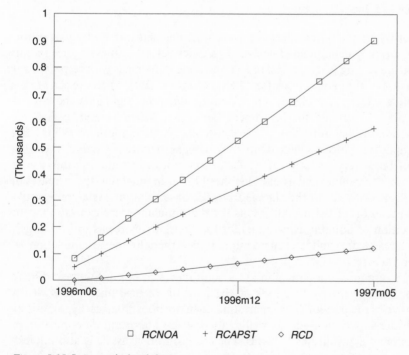

Figure 5.15 Increase in bank loans

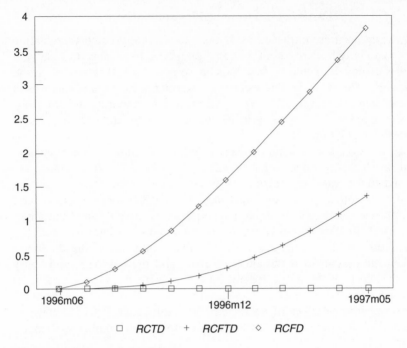

Figure 5.16 Increase in bank loans

deposits) and 5.16 (for effects on zloty time deposits and both types of foreign currency-denominated deposits). A quick review of these figures reveals
some interesting features. The most interesting outcome is with respect to the
response of the capital stock (and hence of investment), where we can see the
positive effect. This clearly unambiguous outcome highlights the role of
liquidity constraints for investment behaviour. When viewed against the
response of the other assets, this outcome is even more revealing. For
example, we notice an increase in zloty demand deposits as well as the other
assets but a very small positive effect, or even no effect at all in the case of
the other three financial assets. One should bear in mind that the increases or
the decreases refer to the change from the base solution. As a conservative
interpretation of the overall results for this simulation, we can say that the
relaxation of liquidity constraints for the Polish firms seems to lead largely
to increases in capital accumulation rather than to the accumulation of
financial assets.

The response to a reduction in the loan rate is shown in Figures 5.17 and
5.18. Once again we first look at the reaction of investment. It is clearly
positive, as expected. It is interesting then to note that, as hypothesized,
both the supply of credit as well as its cost are important determinants of
investment expenditures by firms. The effect on other assets is also interesting. A reduction in the loan rate seems to encourage an increase in the

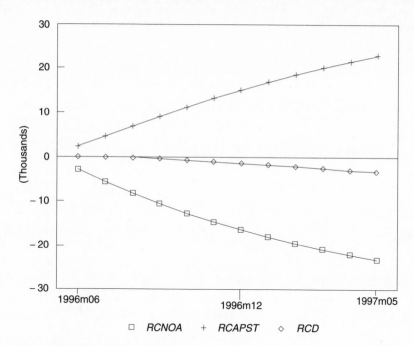

Figure 5.17 Decrease in the loan rate

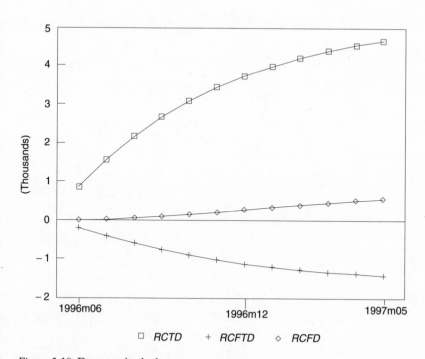

Figure 5.18 Decrease in the loan rate

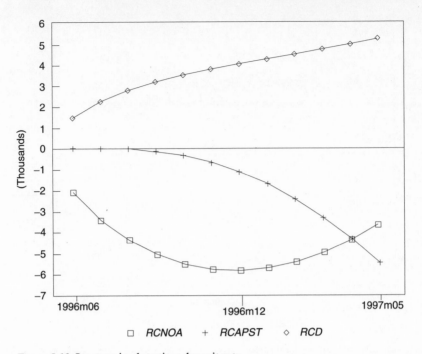

Figure 5.19 Increase in zloty time deposit rate

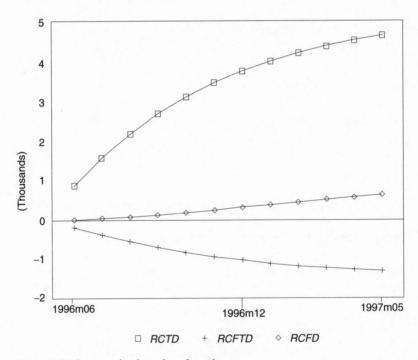

Figure 5.20 Increase in zloty time deposit rate

accumulation of zloty time deposits as well as foreign currency-denominated demand deposits. But, a substitution seems to take place with respect to the other assets and foreign currency-denominated time deposits. Such a reallocation of the portfolio is not surprising, but for our purpose the major outcome is the positive effect on investment.

Finally, the effect of an increase in the rate of interest on the zloty time deposits is shown in Figures 5.19 and 5.20. From Figure 5.19 we can see the negative effect on investment. This is an interesting outcome and is the consequence of our modelling investment expenditure as part of the firm's portfolio behaviour. While the exact mechanism that leads to this result cannot be clear from this partial framework, it is none the less important to note that financial deregulation not only has a direct effect through changes in the quantity and the price of loans to firms, but that other instruments of financial deregulation like the rate of return on financial assets may have a bearing on, albeit indirectly, the firms' portfolio behaviour.

6

THE COMPLETE MODEL[1]

Having developed the models for the household sector, the commercial banking sector and the firm, we will now specify models for the remaining sectors as required by our model and then the full model with the necessary consistency conditions. The missing sectors are the central bank, the government, the external sector and the supply side. To make it easier to understand, the equations and the estimates of the last three chapters are first reproduced along with the necessary definitional relationships left out from those chapters. This task is accomplished in the following section. The chapter ends with some within-sample dynamic simulations for the complete model.

Equations for the commercial banks, the households and the firm

Since the models for households, commercial banks and firms are explained in detail in the previous chapters we can be brief here.

Commercial banks

The budget constraint of the commercial bank is:

$$\Delta RCBNFA = - (\Delta RGOV + \Delta RER + \Delta RL_f - \Delta RCBL) + \Delta RCBNW \quad (6.1)$$

The change in net foreign assets is residually determined via the above budget constraint. The asset demand equations read as:

$$\Delta RL_f = 836769 IF_{-1} - 553534 ICB - 151693\pi - 44248 DEF_{-2} +$$
$$0.168 RCBNW - 0.228 RL_{f,-1} - 0.093 RGOV_{-1} +$$
$$0.140 RCBL_{-1} - 44248 \quad (6.2)$$

$$\Delta RER = 88856\pi + 0.303 RCBNW - 0.319 RL_{f,-1} - 0.175 RGOV_{-1} -$$
$$0.444 RCBNFA_{-1} - 0.873 RER_{-1} + 0.357 RCBL_{-1} \quad (6.3)$$

$$\Delta RGOV = -891342IF_{-1} + 1052396IG - 15288DEF_{-2} +$$
$$0.102RCBNW - 0.219RGOVB_{-1} - 0.184RCBL_{-1} \qquad \textbf{(6.4)}$$

$$\Delta RCBL = 1738423IE + 1284432IG - 826730ICB - 124891\pi +$$
$$11937pe - 0.405RCBNW + 0.482RL_{f,-1} + 0.362RGOV_{-1} +$$
$$0.261RCBNFA_{-1} - 0.697RCBL_{-1} \qquad \textbf{(6.5)}$$

The real stock adjustments are modelled as

$$RL_f = \Delta RL_f + RL_{f,-1} \qquad \textbf{(6.6)}$$

$$RER = \Delta RER + RER_{-1} \qquad \textbf{(6.7)}$$

$$RGOV = \Delta RGOV + RGOVB_{-1} \qquad \textbf{(6.8)}$$

$$RCBL = \Delta RCBL + RCBL_{-1} \qquad \textbf{(6.9)}$$

$$RCBNFA = \Delta RCBNFA + RCBNFA_{-1} \qquad \textbf{(6.10)}$$

Real wealth of commercial banks equals:

$$RCBNW = RZDNS + RFCDNS - RREQRES - RCBNOA \qquad \textbf{(6.11)}$$

The change in real wealth and real net other assets of commercial banks, respectively, per definition is:

$$\Delta RCBNW = RCBNW - RCBNW_{-1} \qquad \textbf{(6.12)}$$

$$\Delta RCBNOA = RCBNOA - RCBNOA_{-1} \qquad \textbf{(6.13)}$$

Zloty and foreign currency-denominated deposits of non-financial sectors, exogenous in Chapter 3, become endogenous in the full model. They are made up of zloty demand and time deposits and foreign currency demand and time deposits, respectively. Both are held by firms and households: i.e.

$$RZDNS = RHD + RHTD + RCD + RCTD \qquad \textbf{(6.14)}$$

$$RFCDNS = RHFD + RHFTD + RCFD + RCFTD \qquad \textbf{(6.15)}$$

Households

The real budget constraint determines the change in net other assets, and is specified as:

$$\Delta RHNOA = Y - C - \Delta RHD - \Delta RHTD - \Delta RHFD - \Delta RHFTD -$$
$$\Delta RHNFA - \Delta RCUR \tag{6.16}$$

Whereas real disposable income of households was exogenous in Chapter 4, it now becomes endogenous. It is specified as:

$$Y = RLABINC + RTR - RHTAX \tag{6.17}$$

where real labour income equals:

$$RLABINC = \frac{W}{P} H \tag{6.18}$$

The equation for real income **(6.17)** shows that we assume that households receive labour income (from firms) and transfers (from the government) and pay taxes (to the government).

The asset demand equations are:

$$\Delta RHFTD = 320556(1 - htaxr)IFTD -$$
$$400895(1 - htaxr)IE + 27674pe \tag{6.19}$$

$$\Delta RHFD = -154740(1 - htaxr)ITD + 1104779(1 - htaxr)IFD -$$
$$782040(1 - htaxr)IFTD + 16579pe + 0.133Y -$$
$$0.051RHFD_{-1} - 0.034RHTD_{-1} \tag{6.20}$$

$$\Delta RHTD = 606183(1 - htaxr)ITD - 64657\pi + 0.127Y$$
$$- 0.144\ RHFTD_{-1} - 0.053RHTD_{-1} - 0.024RHNFA_{-1} \tag{6.21}$$

$$\Delta RHD = 183717(1 - htaxr)ID_{-1} - 437190(1 - htaxr)IE + 0.092Y -$$
$$0.014RHFTD_{-1} - 0.059RCUR_{-1} + 0.002RHNOA_{-1} \tag{6.22}$$

$$\Delta RCUR = -74662\pi + 0.242Y - 0.159RHFD_{-1} - 0.302RCUR_{-1} +$$
$$0.038RHNFA_{-1} + 0.020RHNOA_{-1} \tag{6.23}$$

$$\Delta RHNFA = 0.573RHTD_{-1} - 0.975RHNFA_{-1} - 0.482RHNOA_{-1} +$$
$$268257 \tag{6.24}$$

The equation for real personal consumption is specified as:

$$C = -3707762(1 - htaxr)IFTD + 0.582Y + 0.244RCUR_{-1} +$$
$$0.019RHNFA_{-1} \tag{6.25}$$

and the stock adjustments are modelled as:

$$RHNOA = RHNOA_{-1} + \Delta RHNOA \tag{6.26}$$

$$RHFTD = RHFTD_{-1} + \Delta RHFTD \tag{6.27}$$

$$RHTD = RHTD_{-1} + \Delta RHTD \tag{6.28}$$

$$RHFD = RHFD_{-1} + \Delta RHFD \tag{6.29}$$

$$RHD = RHD_{-1} + \Delta RHD \tag{6.30}$$

$$RCUR = RCUR_{-1} + \Delta RCUR \tag{6.31}$$

$$RHNFA = RHNFA_{-1} + \Delta RHNFA \tag{6.32}$$

Firms

In line with the household sector, the real budget constraint of firms determines the change in real net other assets. It is specified as:

$$\Delta RCNOA = RETAIN - \Delta RCD - \Delta RCTD - \Delta RCFD - \\ \Delta RCFTD - \Delta RCAPST - \Delta RL_f + \Delta RFDI \tag{6.33}$$

Retained earnings, exogenous in Chapter 5, are endogenized by assuming that they are equal to total real sales of goods (which equals total real demand for goods) minus labour income, minus corporate direct taxes. Thus,

$$RETAIN = RTDEM - RLABINC - RCTAX \tag{6.34}$$

It is assumed that profit income is not distributed directly to households. The reason for this assumption is the lack of "data availability." The asset demand equations are:

$$\Delta RCAPST = 0.3595RETAIN + 3884188(1 - ctaxr)IFTD - \\ 674631(1 - ctaxr)IF + 65939\pi + 0.371\Delta RL_f + \\ 1.209\Delta RFDI + 0.0037RCAPST_{-1} - 2.0687RCFD_{-1} \tag{6.35}$$

$$\Delta RCD = 1169369(1 - ctaxr)ID + 523956(1 - ctaxr)ITD - \\ 601268(1 - ctaxr)IK + 95412\pi - 0.0603RCAPST_{-1} - \\ 0.9366RCFD_{-1} + 0.1362RNOA_{-1} + 0.5773RCTD_{-1} - \\ 0.5944RCD_{-1} + 111007 \tag{6.36}$$

$$\Delta RCTD = 308122(1 - ctaxr)ITD - 249348(1 - ctaxr)IF -$$
$$29047\pi - 0.1597RCTD_{-1} + 5675 \tag{6.37}$$

$$\Delta RCFTD = -75694(1 - ctaxr)ITD + 64706(1 - ctaxr)IF +$$
$$2173pe - 0.092RCFTD_{-1} + 0.1094RCFD_{-1} \tag{6.38}$$

$$\Delta RCFD = 58317(1 - ctaxr)IFD + 0.2304\Delta RFDI -$$
$$0.1053RCFTD_{-1} - 0.1340RCFD_{-1} + 0.0012RCNOA_{-1} \tag{6.39}$$

The stock adjustment equations are:

$$RCAPST = \Delta RCAPST + RCAPST_{-1} \tag{6.40}$$

$$RCD = \Delta RCD + RCD_{-1} \tag{6.41}$$

$$RCTD = RCTD_{-1} + \Delta RCTD \tag{6.42}$$

$$RCFTD = \Delta RCFTD + RCFTD_{-1} \tag{6.43}$$

$$RCFD = \Delta RCFD + RCFD_{-1} \tag{6.44}$$

$$RCNOA = \Delta RCNOA + RCNOA_{-1} \tag{6.45}$$

The central bank

It was seen in the chapters on the other three sectors that some of their liabilities and assets originated with the central bank. Those assets and liabilities are now examined in terms of the balance sheet of the Polish central bank (henceforth called the NBP). For this purpose, we first consider the distribution of its assets given in Table 6.1 and graphed in Figure 6.1. The variables are: $RATFA$ for the ratio of central bank gross foreign assets to

Table 6.1 Distribution of assets: NBP (%)

Asset	RATFA	RATLCOMB	RATTGOV	RATOA
Dec. 1991	0.258	0.369	0.222	0.151
Dec. 1992	0.264	0.164	0.415	0.157
Dec. 1993	0.350	0.162	0.408	0.080
Dec. 1994	0.405	0.133	0.370	0.092
Dec. 1995	0.622	0.118	0.175	0.085
May 1996	0.663	0.107	0.154	0.076

Source: Authors' calculations from various issues of the NBP monthly bulletin

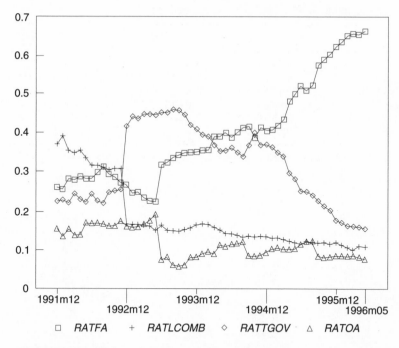

Figure 6.1 Distribution of the assets of the central bank

total assets; *RATLCOMB* for the ratio of NBP lending to commercial banks; *RATTGOV* for total gross lending by the NBP to the central government; and *RATOA* for the ratio of other assets of the NBP. There are a number of striking features in this table and the figure. First, the share of foreign assets has gone up quite substantially, from about 29 per cent in December 1991 to 66 per cent in May 1996. On the other hand, lending to both the commercial banks and the central government has decreased, although the proportional decline of the former is much greater than of the latter. The share of other assets also declined. These trends can be seen much more vividly in Figure 6.1.

As borrowing from the central bank by the central government is an important means of financing the budget deficit, it is also important to look at the distribution of total lending to it by the NBP. This distribution is given in Table 6.2 and Figure 6.2. Here *RATLGOV* stands for the ratio of direct lending by the NBP to the central government; *RATTBILL* gives the ratio of T-bills held by the NBP; and *RATTBONDS* stands for the ratio of bonds held by the NBP. The table divides total lending into three components: direct loans, purchase of T-bills and the purchase of long-term bonds. The most important feature of this table is the sharp reduction in the share of direct loans and the equally important increase in the share of bonds. This

Table 6.2 Distribution of NBP lending to government (%)

Asset	*RATLGOV*	*RATTBILL*	*RATTBONDS*
Dec. 1991	0.568	0.137	0.295
Dec. 1992	0.353	0.345	0.302
Dec. 1993	0.119	0.528	0.353
Dec. 1994	0.089	0.440	0.471
Dec. 1995	0.156	0.003	0.841
May 1996	0.148	0.037	0.817

Source: Authors' calculations from various issues of the NBP monthly bulletin

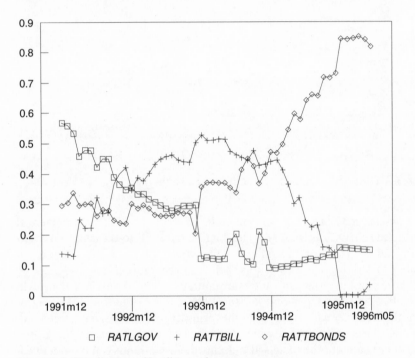

Figure 6.2 Distribution of lending to the government

dramatic turnaround, however, took place at different times for both assets. Direct lending plummeted in 1993 while the purchase of bonds accelerated in 1995. In other words, the share of T-bills remained quite substantial until 1994. These were the consequences of deliberate policies by the central government to finance its budget deficits. The importance of T-bills could, once again, increase as a consequence of the budget law of 1996 according to which the NBP "is obliged to purchase government paper equal in value up to 2% of total budget expenditures in a given fiscal year" (PlanEcon Report, 2 April 1997, p. 12).

We can now look at the liabilities side of the balance sheet. The relevant information is given in Tables 6.3 and 6.4 and Figures 6.3 and 6.4. In these tables and figures, *RATFL* stands for the ratio (as a percentage of total liabilities) of foreign liabilities; *RATTRES* for the ratio of total reserves; *RATCUR* for the ratio of currency; *RATBGOV* for the ratio of liabilities to the government and *RATOLIAB* for the ratio of other liabilities. Further, *RATERES* stands for the ratio of excess reserves to total reserves and *RATREQRES* stands for the ratio of required reserves to total reserves. Leaving aside "other liabilities," variations in the ratios of the remaining liabilities are most obvious in Figure 6.3. The two most important components are the reserves and the currency. The share of the reserves has varied from a low of 16 per cent in December 1994 to a high of 24 per cent in December 1991, while the share of currency varied from 28 per cent in December 1994 to a high of almost 35 per cent in December 1991. These values reflect the changes in the central bank's monetary policy, actions which can be seen by looking at the balance sheets of the households and the commercial banks in particular. Since the implications of changes in the required and the excess reserves are quite different, the composition of the total reserves as given in Table 6.3 and Figure 6.3 is disaggregated in Table 6.4 and Figure 6.4. While the share of required reserves has been normally twice that of the excess reserves, there are considerable variations in these

Table 6.3 Distribution of liabilities: NBP (%)

Liability	RATFL	RATTRES	RATBGOV	RATCUR	RATOLIAB
Dec. 1991	0.070	0.242	0.056	0.347	0.285
Dec. 1992	0.068	0.199	0.044	0.325	0.364
Dec. 1993	0.147	0.176	0.059	0.316	0.302
Dec. 1994	0.188	0.159	0.053	0.280	0.320
Dec. 1995	0.066	0.191	0.052	0.340	0.351
May 1996	0.058	0.202	0.027	0.306	0.407

Source: Authors' calculations from various issues of the NBP monthly bulletin

Table 6.4 Distribution of total reserves (%)

Reserves type	RATERES	RATREQRES
Dec. 1991	0.386	0.614
Dec. 1992	0.404	0.596
Dec. 1993	0.311	0.689
Dec. 1994	0.321	0.679
Dec. 1995	0.361	0.639
May 1996	0.392	0.608

Source: Authors' calculations from various issues of the NBP monthly bulletin

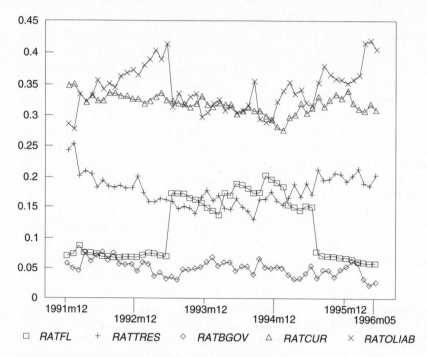

Figure 6.3 Distribution of liabilities of the central bank

shares reflecting considerable variations in the various required reserve ratios by the NBP. As we will see in Chapter 7, changes in the required reserve ratios are one of the NBP's most important instruments of monetary policy.

Based on the above discussion, we model the budget constraint for the central bank thus:

$$\Delta RCUR_s = \Delta RFRES + \Delta RCEBGOV + \Delta RCBL - \Delta RER -$$

$$\Delta RREQRES - \Delta RCEBNOL \tag{6.46}$$

In our model the central bank has a passive role. Most assets and liabilities of the central bank originate from the behaviour of other sectors. $\Delta RFRES$ is determined via the balance of payments; $\Delta RCEBGOV$ is residually determined via the budget constraint of the government (see below); $\Delta RCBL$ and ΔRER are determined via the commercial banking sector (see above); $\Delta RCEBNOL$ is exogenous. The budget constraint of the NBP determines $\Delta RCUR_s$.

The NBP sets required reserve ratios, which determine the absolute amount of required reserves. Hence:

$$RREQRES = rat_1(RHD + RCD) + rat_2(RHTD + RCTD) +$$

$$rat_3(RHFD + RCFD) + rat_4(RHFTD + RCFTD) \tag{6.47}$$

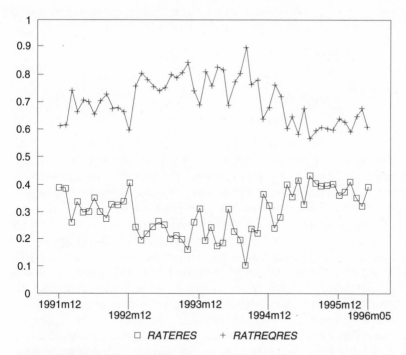

Figure 6.4 Distribution of reserves

The NBP also determines the exchange rate. In Poland, the exchange rate is traditionally determined via a crawling peg system. In May 1995 the system of setting the zloty rate changed somewhat. The current system implies a partial flotation of the zloty within a 7-percent band of a fixed daily rate (see the PlanEcon Report, 30 September 1995). In our complete model it is assumed that the exchange rate is set on the basis of domestic price behaviour. Moreover, expected relative changes in the nominal exchange rate are assumed to be equal to actual relative changes in the nominal exchange rate. We use the following equation in the full model:

$$pe = 0.729\pi_{-1}$$

$$(5.48) \; adj. \, R^2 = 0.15 \qquad\qquad\qquad\qquad\qquad \textbf{(6.48)}$$

This equation is based on an OLS regression using actual monthly data for the period December 1991–May 1996 (t-value below coefficient).

Using the above equation the level of the nominal exchange rate is determined as:

$$EXCHR = (1 + pe)EXCHR_{-1} \qquad\qquad\qquad\qquad \textbf{(6.49)}$$

Assuming that foreign prices are constant, the real exchange rate is modelled as:

$$REXCHR = \frac{EXCHR}{P} \qquad (6.50)$$

The government sector

As we saw in the balance sheets of the commercial banks and the central bank, the government borrows significantly from these two sectors to finance its expenditures (because of running budget deficits). The implications of this feature for financial policy can be best understood by looking at the budget constraint of the Polish central government. Some data on this are given in Table 6.5. It gives the shares of the different instruments to finance government expenditures. The table provides data on very broad aggregates and not on the type of disaggregates given in the balance sheet of the NBP, that is, in terms of the breakdown in terms of T-bills and long-term bonds. But even from these broad aggregates, we can see some interesting features of the Polish government's fiscal behaviour as far as its implications for financial policy are concerned. Two points stand out: they are the declining importance of the NBP to finance budget deficits, although, as pointed out above, this could change due to the new budget law; the second is the increasing role of commercial bank borrowing. The latter, as is well known, leads to the crowding out of private loans by government loans, which could have serious consequences for an economy like that of Poland where economic agents tend to be credit-constrained.

Be that as it may, the budget constraint of the central government in our full model is modelled as:

$$\Delta RCEBGOV = RGOVCON + RTR - RHTAX - RCTAX - \Delta RGOV -$$

$$\Delta RFDEBT - \Delta RGNOL \qquad (6.51)$$

Personal and corporate taxes are modelled as:

Table 6.5 Financing of government expenditures by instrument (%)

Instrument	1992	1993	1994	1995
Borrowing from NBP	0.20	0.05	0.05	−0.10
Borrowing from commercial banks	0.09	0.14	0.13	0.12
Direct taxes	0.33	0.32	0.35	0.36
Other revenues	0.38	0.50	0.46	0.61

Source: Authors' calculations from various issues of the NBP monthly bulletin

$$RHTAX = htaxr\ RLABINC \qquad\qquad (6.52)$$

$$RCTAX = ctaxr(RTDEM - RLABINC) \qquad\qquad (6.53)$$

Real government consumption is modelled as a fixed share of total sales of goods (equals total demand for goods):

$$RGCON = share\ RSAL \qquad\qquad (6.54)$$

The external sector

Capital flows between Poland and other countries are, in our model, partly determined via the asset demand equations of the different domestic sectors, but they are also partly exogenous. Total capital flows consist of net foreign asset holdings by households and commercial banks (see equations above), foreign borrowing by the government and foreign direct investments used as a financing item by firms (both are exogenous), net other capital flows and the change in foreign reserves. Abstracting from interest payments, the balance of payments is modelled as:

$$\Delta RFRES = RTRADEB - \Delta RHNFA - \Delta RCBNFA - \Delta REXNOA +$$

$$\Delta RFDI + \Delta RFDEBT \qquad\qquad (6.55)$$

The change in foreign reserves is residually determined via the balance of payments equation. The stock of foreign reserves then equals:

$$RFRES = RFRES_{-1} + \Delta RFRES \qquad\qquad (6.56)$$

The "real" trade balance, denominated in constant domestic prices and exchange rates, is modelled as simply as possible. We assume that the trade balance is determined by the real exchange rate and the total demand for goods (approximated in the estimates by real GDP). The equation we use is:

$$RTRADEB = 0.397 REXCHR - 0.081 RTDEM + 0.579 RTRADEB_{-1}$$
$$\qquad\quad (2.85) \qquad\qquad (-3.22) \qquad\qquad (5.95);$$

$$adj.\ R^2 = 0.48 \qquad\qquad (6.57)$$

This equation is based on an OLS regression using Polish monthly data for December 1991–May 1996. The t-values are given below the coefficients.

The (change in) net other assets held by the external sector is determined residually by the following equation.

$$\Delta REXNOA = \Delta RCBNOA + \Delta RHNOA + \Delta RCNOA -$$

$$\Delta RCEBNOL - \Delta RGNOL \qquad (6.58)$$

This equation says that net other assets (net other assets of all domestic sectors minus net other liabilities of all domestic sectors) should, per definition, be equal to net other assets held by foreigners.

The supply side

The supply side in our model is also modelled as simply as possible. We assume that real production is determined by a Cobb–Douglas production function in labour and capital. We have not tried to estimate the production function, but rather used the average labour share in production (calculated by using our data set) as the elasticity with respect to labour. The actual equation used is:

$$RPROD = 0.006H^{0.712}RCAPST^{0.288} \qquad (6.59)$$

The shift parameter, which equals 0.006, is determined by calibrating the Cobb–Douglas production function for May 1996.

The determination of the real capital stock is already explained above. The demand for labour, given the real capital stock, has to be set out. An important aspect of the former socialist economies, including Poland, is the role of working-capital credit (see Calvo and Kumar, 1994). In many of these countries wages have to be paid at the beginning of the production process. Given the fact that initial liquidity is unavailable, firms need to borrow from banks to be able to hire labour. Ideally, therefore, our model should consider the flow of working-capital credit between commercial banks and firms, which is used by the firms to hire workers. However, the data on loans to firms we are aware of, do not distinguish between loans for working capital and loans for fixed capital. Moreover, our model assumes that there are no lags between hiring labourers, production, sale of goods and receipts from the sale of goods. Therefore, this approach could not be followed. In order to take into account, in some way, the working-capital issue, which is indeed important in Poland, we took the following approach. Assuming a Cobb–Douglas production function demand for labour is normally derived by equating the marginal productivity of labour to the real wage rate. However, when labour expenses have to be financed before production takes place, and all of the advanced labour expenses have to be financed by bank loans, the labour costs per worker actually equal the real wage rate times one plus the loan rate. Therefore, we basically derive labour demand by equating the marginal productivity of labour to the real wage rate adjusted for the loan rate.

Actually, by not explicitly modelling flows of working capital, we assume that households, who receive their wage bill in advance, immediately use these advances to buy goods from firms, which in turn use these receipts for buying investment goods and financial assets. This implies that credit which is earmarked for working capital immediately flows back to firms in the form of receipts from the sale of goods.

The equation for labour demand which is used in the model is derived by an OLS regression using monthly data for December 1991–May 1996, and reads as:

$$H = 17.74 RTDEM_{-3} - 483219907 \left(\frac{W(1 + IF)}{P}\right)_{-3} + 0.63 H_{-4} + 5809202$$
$$\quad (2.5) \qquad\qquad (-1.80) \qquad\qquad\qquad\qquad (7.39) \qquad (3.52)$$

$$adj. R^2 = 0.71 \tag{6.60}$$

The t-values are given below the coefficients. In the estimates *RTDEM* (which equals real sales of goods) is approximated by real GDP.[2]

Prices and wages

Nominal wages are determined by a Philips curve-like equation. The equation is estimated for the period December 1991–May 1996, and reads as:

$$PW = -0.0056(UNR - UNR_{-1}) + 1.006\pi_{-2} + 0.007$$
$$\quad (-2.00) \qquad\qquad\qquad (1.67) \qquad (0.40)$$

$$adj. R^2 = 0.08 \tag{6.61}$$

The nominal wage rate is then modelled as:

$$W = (1 + PW)W_{-1} \tag{6.62}$$

The unemployment rate equals:

$$UNR = \frac{(LABF - H)}{LABF} \tag{6.63}$$

With respect to the clearing of the goods market, we have several options. First, the model could be used assuming that the goods market is continuously cleared by price changes. In that case for each period the real production of goods equals real demand for goods and hence equals real GDP. A second option is to assume sluggishness in prices, thus allowing for differences between the production of goods and real demand for goods (sales). In that case real changes in stocks equilibrate the goods market. We have experimented with both options. What was quite interesting was the fact that with respect to the behaviour of the model, both approaches gave, *on average*, almost identical results for all endogenous variables. That is to say, correcting for cyclical behaviour, the trend in the variables is almost identical. However, with respect to the behaviour in *each* period, the first option leads to a much higher variability of inflation, both as compared to the actual variability of inflation as well as to the simulated variability of inflation. This high variability of inflation causes a much higher fluctuation per period in the other endogenous variables as compared to the fluctuation per period of the endogenous variables using the second option. Of course, this result may not come as a surprise since, when using the second option, the fluctuation is taken into account by changes in real stocks, which do not directly affect other variables in the model. In the remainder of this chapter, and also for the next chapter, we have run the model assuming sluggishness in prices.

The necessary equations, then, are as follows. Total real production (supply of goods) is as explained above. The total demand for goods, which equals total sales, is modelled as the demand for goods by firms, the government and households, plus the real trade balance. Hence:

$$TRDEM = C + RGOVCON + RTRADEB \tag{6.64}$$

Prices are then determined as:

$$P = P_{-1} - 0.000005RSTOCK \tag{6.65}$$

The coefficient is set by doing different simulation experiments, in which we try to replicate the actual behaviour of the price level. In these simulations the starting value of $RSTOCK$ is set at zero. The simulation results were reasonable, and also quite similar, for a coefficient between 0.000010 and 0.000001. Coefficients outside this range gave unreasonable results. We choose the average in the actual simulations.

The real stock of goods equals:

$$RSTOCK = RSTOCK_{-1} + RPROD - TRDEM \tag{6.66}$$

and the rate of inflation is derived by:

$$\pi = \frac{(P - P_{-1})}{P} \tag{6.67}$$

The complete model

Table 6.6 presents the entire model in the form of a flow of funds system. The different columns specify the budget constraints of the sectors. In the first row the real side of the model is given. A positive variable is a receipt, a negative variable a payment. For firms the change in the capital stock (investment) is included along with the expenditures on the real side of the model. The sum of the real side gives the goods market equilibrium condition. The other rows specify the financial side, i.e., the change in assets and liabilities of the different sectors. A positive variable is an asset, a negative variable a liability.

The market equilibrium conditions can be derived from Table 6.6. For most cases one side of the market determines the outcome. Two markets are not cleared by either the demand or the supply side. The first one is the goods market, which is cleared by either the price of goods or by changes in stocks. In the latter case, the equilibrium condition reads as:

$$RPROD = RTDEM + \Delta RSTOCK = C + RGOVCON + RTRADEB +$$
$$\Delta RSTOCK = RGDP \qquad \textbf{(6.68)}$$

However, if the first option is used, the market equilibrium condition reads:

$$RPROD = RTDEM = C + RGOVCON + RTRADEB = RGDP \qquad \textbf{(6.69)}$$

The second one is the market for currency. Due to Walras's Law, the latter is automatically in equilibrium, given the explicit modelling of all budget constraints. Hence, the condition is not modelled explicitly.[3]

A complete list of the endogenous and the exogenous variables and their exact definitions is given in the Appendix to this chapter.

Some within-sample dynamic simulations

While our estimated model is not meant as a forecasting tool, it is none the less useful to judge the quality of its tractability of the actual data, just as we have done with the partial models in the previous chapters. In this case it is even more important because we wish to use the full model for policy simulations. It would be arduous and cumbersome to report the time path of all of the endogenous variables. Therefore, we follow a rather selective approach and report the results for four of the variables in the text and a few other variables from each of the sectors in the Appendix to this chapter. While the reader can judge for the quality of the "fit" of the variables in the Appendix, we do offer some brief comments on the outcome with respect to the four variables reported in the text.

The first variable is the capital stock, and the time path of the simulated

Table 6.6 Flow of funds of the entire model

Commercial banks	Household	Firm	Central Bank	Government	External Sector	Total
	RLABINC+RTR −RHTAX−C	TRDEM−RLABINC −RCTAX−ΔRCAPST		RHTAX+RCTAX −RTR−RGOVCON	−RTRADEB	TRDEM=C+ RGOVCON +RTRADEB
ΔRGOV				−ΔRGOV		0
ΔRER			−ΔRER			0
$ΔRL_f$		$−ΔRL_f$				0
−ΔRCBL			ΔRCBL			0
ΔRCBNFA	ΔRHNFA	−ΔRFDI	ΔRFRES	−ΔRFDEBT	* HELP	0
−ΔRHD	ΔRHD					0
−ΔRHTD	ΔRHTD					0
−ΔRHFD	ΔRHFD					0
−ΔRHFTD	ΔRHFTD					0
−ΔRCD		ΔRCD				0
−ΔRCTD		ΔRCTD				0
−ΔRCFD		ΔRCFD				0
−ΔRCFTD		ΔRCFTD				0
ΔRREQRES			−ΔRREQRES			0
ΔRCBNOA	ΔRHNOA	ΔRCNOA	−ΔRCEBNOL	−ΔRGNOL	−ΔRECNOA	0
	ΔRCUR		$ΔRCUR_s$			0
			ΔRCEBGOV	−ΔRCEBGOV		0
0	0	0	0	0	0	0

* where $HELP = − (ΔRCBNFA+ΔRHNFA+ΔRFRES)+ΔRFDI+ΔRFDEBT$

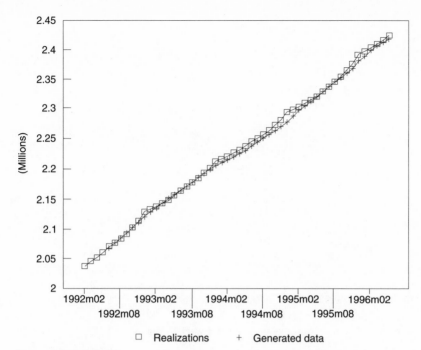

Figure 6.5 RCAPST

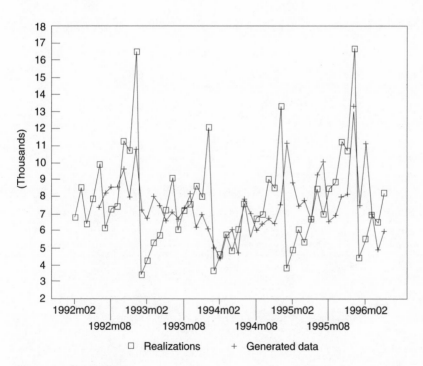

Figure 6.6 DRCAPST

105

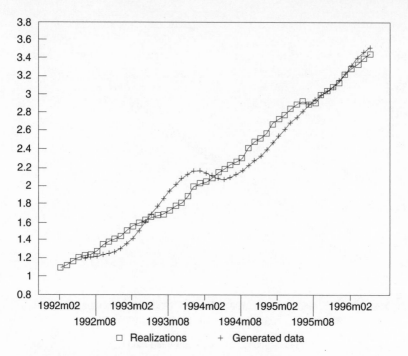

Figure 6.7 P

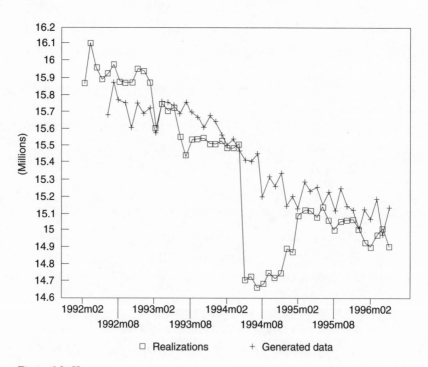

Figure 6.8 H

and the actual values is given in Figure 6.5. The closeness of the fit in this case is obvious. But, as can be expected, the outcome with respect to its flow counterpart is less dramatic (see Figure 6.6). However, even here the simulated values track the direction of the changes quite well.

The last two simulations relate to the price level in Figure 6.7 and the level of employment in Figure 6.8. In both cases the outcome is reasonably acceptable. Of course, in both cases the simulated values sometimes under-estimate and sometimes overestimate the actual values, but in no case are there such drastic variations as to completely render the outcome meaningless.

What is quite heartening about these simulations, as well as those not reported, is that they are the result of a model that is based on less than perfect data and which cannot claim to capture every aspect of the Polish economy. It would thus seem that our estimated model can be used, with a reasonable degree of assurance, for the kind of policy simulations that we will report in Chapter 7.

7

SOME POLICY SIMULATIONS

As mentioned before, one of the main goals of this monograph is to use the model specified and estimated in the previous chapters to carry out some policy simulations of some of the main indicators of financial reforms in Poland. For this purpose we concentrate on those instruments of policy that are either most frequently used by the National Bank of Poland, or by the commercial banks, or are major indicators of such reforms.

With these as the selection criteria in mind, we will concentrate on the effects of changes in the discount rate, required reserve ratios, the commercial bank loan and default rates and the deposit rates. Although the loan default rates are not an instrument of policy *per se*, they are none the less subject to control by the commercial banks to some extent in the sense that the banks can do a better job of assessing the risks of potential borrowers by improving the qualities of their loan officers, for example. Consequently, we also examine the effects of changes in the default rates.[1]

Effects of changes in the discount rate

The NBP has used its lending rate to the commercial banks as an important tool of monetary policy. Before 1996, the central bank's lending rates consisted of: the rediscount rate, the Lombard rate and the refinance rate. However, as of early 1997, the refinance rate ceased to be one of the lending rates. As an example, as of 17 July 1997, the lending rates were: rediscount rate (22 per cent) and the Lombard rate (25 per cent). Our simulations are intended as a means of examining rather broad issues here: What are the consequences of reducing the discount rate on some of the main macro variables?

The effects of discount rate changes can be analyzed under a number of different assumptions. For example, we can first assume that it only affects commercial bank borrowings, but leaves the deposit and the loan rates unchanged. An alternative assumption would be to model the interdependence between the central bank discount rate and the commercial bank loan and deposit rates. In this section, we examine both scenarios.

It has been suggested that the commercial banks in Poland set their deposit rates with reference to the national bank lending rate according to some sort of a reaction function (see, e.g., Ebrill et al., 1994, p. 30). While there can be many possible specifications of the underlying reaction function, we have used a rather simple one to capture the basic elements of the dependence. Since there are four deposit rates and one loan rate considered, we have estimated five reaction functions. The results are given below:

$$ID = 0.023ICB_{-1} + 0.087ID_{-1}$$
$$(1.92) \qquad (13.98) \qquad R^2\text{: } 0.74 \tag{7.1}$$

$$ITD = 0.072ICB_{-1} + 0.903ITD_{-1}$$
$$(1.35) \qquad (14.42) \qquad R^2\text{: } 0.95 \tag{7.2}$$

$$IFD = 0.015ICB_{-1} + 0.805IFD_{-1}$$
$$(2.35) \qquad (14.42) \qquad R^2\text{: } 0.87 \tag{7.3}$$

$$IFTD = 0.010ICB_{-1} + 0.903IFTD_{-1}$$
$$(1.57) \qquad (20.30) \qquad R^2\text{: } 0.94 \tag{7.4}$$

$$IF = 0.042ICB_{-1} + 0.950IF_{-1}$$
$$(0.95) \qquad (21.94) \qquad R^2\text{: } 0.98 \tag{7.5}$$

These reaction functions give plausible results, suggesting that changes in the discount rate lead to changes in the various deposit and the loan rates in the same direction as expected. However, they also suggest that the relationship is not necessarily instantaneous, thus confirming the actual experience as spelled out in the previous quotations from the NBP.

The effects of the changes in the discount rate under the two alternate assumptions are given in Figures 7.1 to 7.4. We have simulated the effects of a decrease of the discount rate by 25 per cent. The lines, as before, represent deviations from the base run. While in principle we can simulate the effects on all of the endogenous variables, here we follow a highly selective approach. We concentrate only on those variables that we can expect to behave in certain ways on a priori grounds and a few of the main macro variables. Thus, for this set of simulations, we selected four variables: commercial bank loans to firms, commercial bank borrowings from the central bank, the capital stock and the price level. All other things being equal, we should expect the supply of loans to increase. This expectation is confirmed in Figure 7.1. What is, however, interesting is that the two scenarios do yield different results, as one might expect. The increase in the supply of bank loans to firms, as measured from the base, is somewhat less

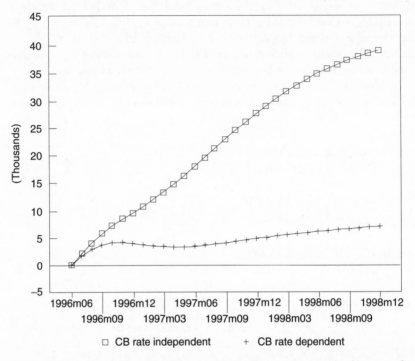

Figure 7.1 Decrease in the discount rate (25%): effect on the supply of loans to firms

when the various deposit and the lending rates respond to the central bank discount rate. This would seem to suggest that as the Polish money market becomes more efficient where the commercial banks react much more quickly to changes in the discount rate, the outcome represented by the alternate scenario would become the norm and, therefore, the ability of the discount rate changes to affect loan supply by commercial banks will be somewhat reduced.

Figure 7.2 shows the effect on commercial bank borrowings from the central bank. In this case, we should expect an increase under both scenarios, which is precisely what we find. In a way, the outcome in Figure 7.1 is really a mirror image of the outcome in Figure 7.2. As commercial borrowings increase, so does the loan supply. Again, we can see that the rate-dependent effect is less marked than the rate-independent case. The outcomes in the two figures are thus consistent with each other. What is remarkable about these two simulations is that the outcome is very textbook-like.

Next, we consider the effects on two macro variables: capital stock and the price level. The behaviour of the capital stock, of course, reflects the response of investment, while the behaviour of the price level reflects the outcome of the various effects on both the aggregate demand and the aggregate supply sides. In Figure 7.3 we can see that for both scenarios the effect is

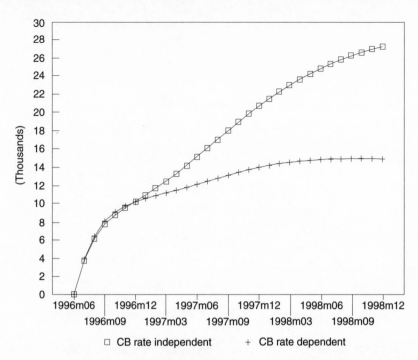

Figure 7.2 Decrease in the discount rate (25%): effect on commercial bank borrowing

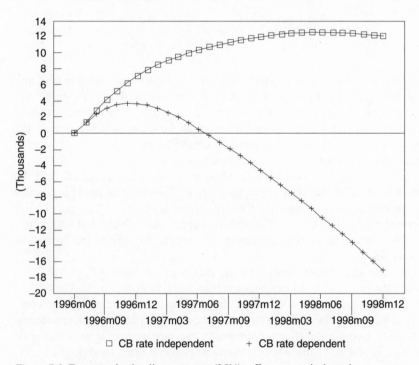

Figure 7.3 Decrease in the discount rate (25%): effect on capital stock

111

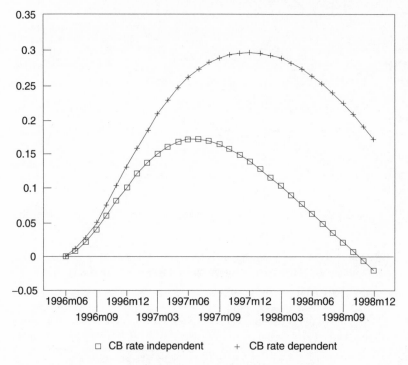

Figure 7.4 Decrease in the discount rate (25%): effect on prices

positive, at least for the initial period. This is a plausible outcome in response to a reduction in the central bank discount rate and is consistent with the effect on the supply of loans to firms in Figure 7.1. However, it should be noted that the effect on the capital stock becomes negative during the simulation period in the rate-dependent case. The effect on the price level in Figure 7.4 would appear to be consistent with the outcomes shown in the previous three figures. What is interesting in this case is that the effect of the two scenarios diverges after about six months. The effect on prices is positive for the initial period, suggesting that demand side effects of the central bank discount rate policy may well dominate supply side effects. But ultimately, the effect becomes smaller, suggesting that supply side effects are starting to play a role.

The simulations with respect to the effects of changes in the NBP's discount rate would seem to suggest that they work in expected ways in Poland and further that the dependence of the various rates of return of the commercial banks on the discount rate may have significant implications for the quantitative size of the effects. Our results also emphasize the importance of the lags in the response of the commercial bank rates to changes in the central bank rate.

Effects of changes in required reserve ratios

As of February 1994 commercial banks have been required to keep reserves against all four types of deposits with the National Bank of Poland. The required reserve ratios have been systematically used as a powerful instrument of monetary policy by the NBP. For example, as recently as 28 February 1997 the NBP announced that the "obligatory reserve levels for commercial banks would be increased." Obligatory reserves for zloty call deposits rose from 17 per cent to 20 per cent, and foreign currency deposits from 2 per cent to 4 per cent. According to the NBP, the main reason behind this move was an unexpected sale to the NBP by the Ministry of Finance of Treasury bills worth 2.5 billion zlotys. The proceeds from the sale were to be used to make additional payments for health and education services. According to the budget law for 1996, the NBP had to purchase these securities if no other buyers were forthcoming. The consequences of such a move for the 1997 monetary policy guidelines were, however, obviously negative; this obliged the NBP to take ameliorative measures (PlanEcon Report, 2 April 1997, p. 10). The reserve ratios have also been used quite frequently. For example, quite apart from the changes noted in the above quotation, the required ratios for some of the earlier periods were as shown in Table 7.1.

What is obvious from the brief discussion above and the table is that the required reserve ratios have been used not only as the standard tool of monetary management, but have also been used to neutralize the effects of governments' temptations to use the bank to instantaneously monetize its deficits. But it is also clear from the various values of the ratios that they are changed far more frequently, and the magnitude of the changes is much greater than one would find in more developed banking systems. That such major changes in required reserve ratios can have serious consequences on the loan portfolios of the commercial banks and on the supply of loans to firms and households goes without saying. In the simulations reported below, this is precisely the issue we wish to address.

It should be noticed from Table 7.1 that not only are the ratios different for different deposits, but also that the relative changes in the required reserve ratios for deposits in the two types of currency change in varying magnitudes. So, the questions that we want to ask are: what would be the effects of

Table 7.1 Required reserve ratios (%)

	March 1995	*June 1996*
Zloty demand deposits	20	17
Zloty time deposits	9	9
Foreign currency demand deposits	1	2
Foreign currency time deposits	1	2

Source: Various issues of NBP Information Bulletins

the same proportionate, say, reduction, in the required reserve ratio of one of the deposits at a time? What would happen if all such requirements were abolished from the foreign currency-denominated deposits? The point is that there does not seem to be any well-articulated rationale for the observed levels and changes in the four ratios, so it would be useful to have some idea as to the consequences of changes in these ratios.

In this section, then, we carry out simulations with respect to two sets of changes in the required reserve ratios: those relating to the foreign currency-denominated deposits and those on zloty demand deposits. The rationale for the first is that in the earlier period covered by this study there were no requirements of reserves on the foreign currency deposits and so we would like to find out what would happen if we were to go back to that practice. The rationale for the second set of simulations is that the required reserve ratio on zloty demand deposits is very high, as can be seen from Table 7.1, and it would be interesting to see the consequences of reducing it to levels more in common with the developed countries' central banking practices. As for the variables selected to show the effects, we concentrate on two: commercial bank loans to firms and excess reserve holdings by the commercial banks.

Figure 7.5 shows the effect of abolishing all of the reserve requirements on

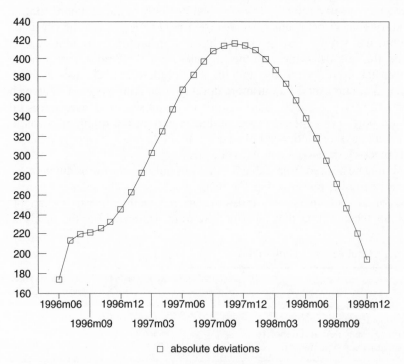

Figure 7.5 Abolish reserves on foreign deposits: effect on bank loans to firms

the foreign currency deposits on the supply of loans to firms. The behaviour is like an inverted U-shape, suggesting that initially the effect on loan supply to firms is positive, reaching a peak and then declining. The effect on excess reserves is shown in Figure 7.6. Here the effect is initially also positive, but it then starts a continuous decline. It is important to remember that these effects are in terms of deviations from the base run. The effects of a decline in the required reserve ratio on zloty demand deposits of 25 per cent are shown in Figure 7.7 on loans to firms, and in Figure 7.8 on excess reserves. Figure 7.7 shows that a decrease in the reserve requirement ratio on zloty demand deposits would seem to lead to an increase in the supply of loans to firms over the whole period simulated, thus indicating a more systematically positive effect than in the case of removing the reserve requirements from the foreign currency deposits. The effect on excess reserves, on the other hand, is less marked than on the supply of loans and does not seem to be too pronounced.

Our results with respect to the effects of changes in the various required reserve ratios are thus quite revealing. They clearly show that the high required reserve ratios have succeeded in draining off liquidity from the commercial banking system, thus reducing its loan base significantly.

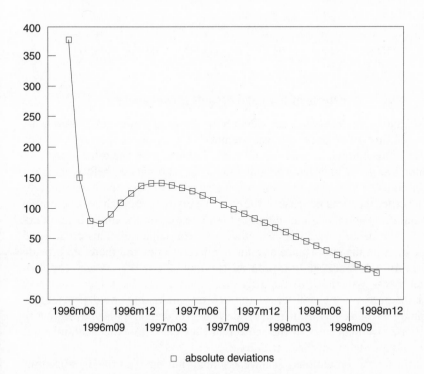

□ absolute deviations

Figure 7.6 Abolish reserves on foreign deposits: effect on excess reserves

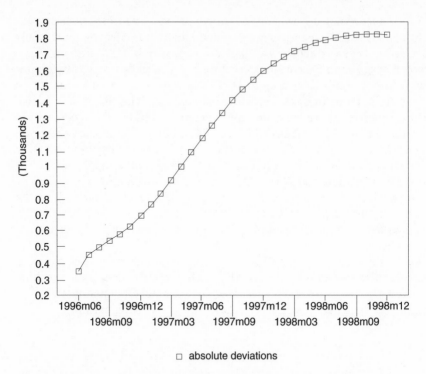

□ absolute deviations

Figure 7.7 Decrease in reserves on zloty deposits (25%): effect on loans to firms

Effects of loan and default rate changes

As we have seen, loan rates can affect both the supply of credit as well as its cost and thus affect both aggregate demand and supply. A special feature of the Polish economy, as we have seen, in common with the other transition economies, is the high loan default rate. This, as discussed before, means a lower effective loan rate. One interesting experiment here, then, would be to see whether the same increase in the effective loan rate brought about, on the one hand, by an increase in the gross loan rate and on the other, by a reduction in the default rate, will have the same consequences. This could shed some light on the importance of reducing default rates and therefore provide some rationale for expenditures on the training of loan officers who can then better assess loan risks. To the extent that commercial bank loan rates may be influenced by the policies of the central bank, this could provide the commercial banks with an independent instrument of policy to influence their effective loan rates in the sense that they can affect their default rates quite independently of the central bank.

In the above simulations, we have assumed that the loan rate is exogenous and that the default rate acts directly to change the effective loan rate. We

116

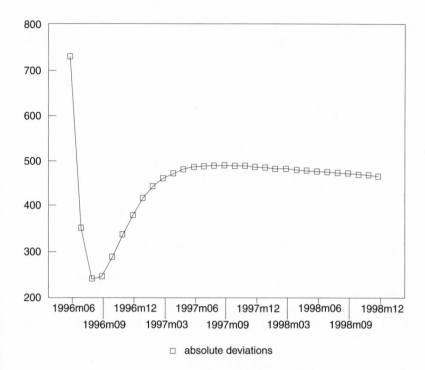

□ absolute deviations

Figure 7.8 Decrease in reserves on zloty deposits (25%): effect on excess reserves

can also model the effect of a reduction in the default rate differently. In this case the loan rate equals the deposit rate and a mark-up; the mark-up is then determined by the default rate, amongst other variables. In this case the gross loan rate becomes endogenous. More formally, to carry out this simulation about the effect of changes in the default rate, we proceed as follows. Define

$$IF = ITD + spread \qquad\qquad (7.6)$$

where *spread* is the mark-up. The use of the *IF* and the *ITD* need some explanation. Remember that we have not included commercial bank loans to households in the analysis for reasons already explained. Therefore, we are modelling only the loan rate to firms. As for the use of the rate on the zloty time deposits, we assume that the commercial banks determine the spread with respect to the highest rate on their liabilities, which happens to be the zloty time deposits.

Ideally, the spread should be modelled as being dependent on all required reserves and default rate (see, for example, Ebrill *et al.*, 1994, p. 31), but preliminary estimates showed that there was very high collinearity between

117

the four ratios, and that all four ratios turned out to be insignificant, with quite a few having wrong signs. Consequently we modelled the spread as follows:

$$spread = 0.083 rat_2 + 0.0136 DEF - 0.0071$$
$$\quad\quad (1.46) \quad\quad (1.68) \quad\quad (-1.53) \quad\quad R^2 = 0.17 \quad\quad\quad (7.7)$$

where rat_2 is the required reserve ratio on zloty time deposits and DEF is the default rate. Both coefficients are positive, which accords with our *a priori* expectations. In other words, the results suggest that the higher the required reserve ratio and the default rates, the higher the spread and, with a given deposit rate, the higher the gross loan rate.

In these simulations, two variables are considered: loans to firms by commercial banks and the capital stock. The effects of an increase in the gross loan rate versus a decrease in the default rate, so that both changes lead to the same increase in the effective loan rate (a 15 per cent increase), are shown in Figure 7.9. It is clear that the effect is essentially the same qualitatively in both cases, as we should expect: namely, that the supply of loans increases, but the effect is more pronounced where the effective rate is increased by reducing the default rate. This may have interesting implications for com-

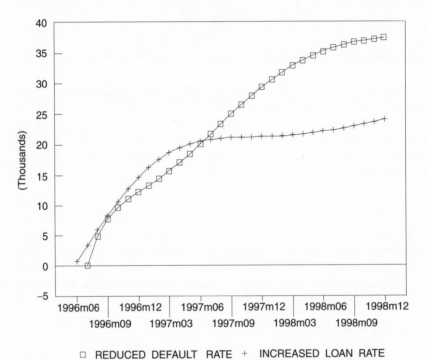

Figure 7.9 Increase in the effective loan rate: effect on the supply of loans to firms

118

mercial bank behaviour in terms of its loan rate policies and may suggest that more attention should be paid to the issue of the high default rates.

The importance of this simulation is brought out equally sharply when we look at Figure 7.10, which shows the effect on the capital stock. In this case the effect is all the more positive when the effective rate is increased via reduction in the default rate, which is not the case when the desired increase is brought about by an increase in the gross loan rate. This is not all that surprising because when the gross loan rate goes up, the cost of loans goes up, which may have a detrimental effect on investment. This, of course, is not the case when the default rate decreases. Once again, we can see how import-ant it can be to reduce the high loan default rates.

The next two simulations in this section are devoted to the effects of a reduction in the default rate: one direct, as in the above two simulations, and one where the effect comes via the dependence of the spread on the default rate. Consider then Figure 7.11. It shows the effect on the supply of bank loans to firms. We can notice a number of interesting things from this figure. For one thing, both methods of examining the effect of the reduction in the default rate lead to the same qualitative results, although a mild decline is suggested towards the end of the period in the case where the loan rate becomes endogenous. The second important point is that the effect is more

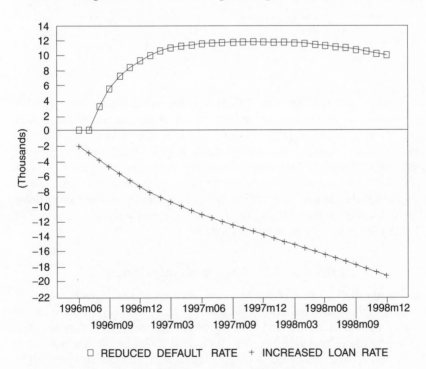

Figure 7.10 Increase in the effective loan rate: effect on capital stock

119

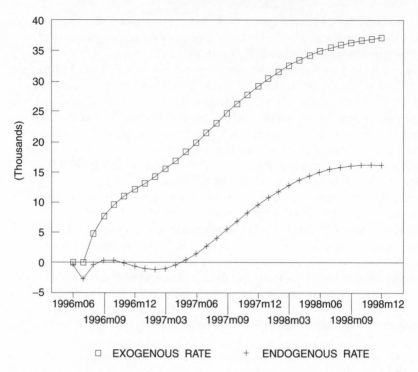

Figure 7.11 Decrease in the default rate: 2 mechanisms (effect on the supply of bank loans)

pronounced when the loan rate is treated as an exogenous variable without any dependence on the default rate. In terms of the effects on the capital stock, the results are given in Figure 7.12. The main result, which is that both lead to an increase in the capital stock, is quite clear, but the somewhat greater effect when the loan rate is endogenous may seem counter to what Figure 7.11 says. However, it should be noted that when the loan rate is endogenous, the default rate affects both the effective and the gross loan rates, and it is quite possible that the two effects could work in such a way as to lead to the seemingly counter result.

Effects of zloty time deposit rate changes

Considering the structure of interest rates on the various deposits, we recall that the nominal rates were the highest on the zloty time deposits. But, if we consider the real rate, we find that all except the zloty time deposits had negative real rates and even the zloty time deposits had quite low real rates. This would seem to be almost a case of financial repression. But one might argue that the rates on demand deposits are normally non-existent even in

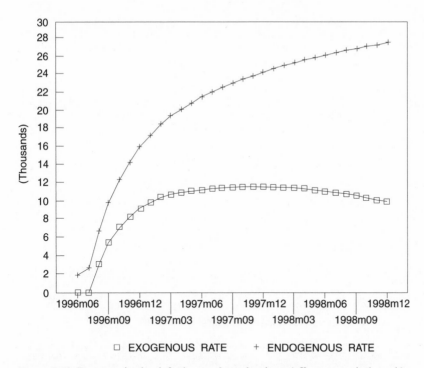

Figure 7.12 Decrease in the default rate: 2 mechanisms (effect on capital stock)

the most developed financial markets, and that the return on foreign currency deposits *per se* are not important. Since the latter are held more as an inflation hedge with an eye on the behaviour of the exchange rates, the only rate worth looking at is the zloty time deposit rate. And it is only with respect to this rate that we can say that a condition akin to financial repression may be said to exist.

The effects of this simulation are examined in terms of the changes in the portfolios of both the households and the firms. We consider an increase in the rate of 25 per cent. Figure 7.13 gives the effect on the portfolio of the households. It considers all five financial assets. The first to be considered, of course, is the behaviour of zloty time deposits. It can be seen that the share of this asset goes up. There would appear to be substitution against the two foreign currency-denominated deposits, but the share of currency goes up. These changes are particularly significant given the importance of foreign currency deposits in the households' portfolio and in fact in the Polish economy in general.

Since consumption is modelled as an integral part of the portfolio model, it is also useful to consider the effect on it. The results are given in Figure 7.14. After an initial reduction, it goes up, with reference to the base period. While it is difficult to say what mechanisms are exactly working here, none

121

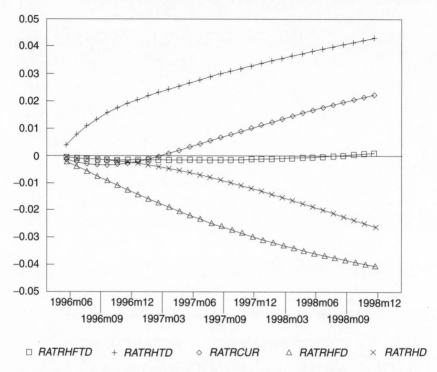

Figure 7.13 Increase in the zloty time deposit rate (25%): effect on households portfolio

the less the initial decline is unsurprising, for in this case the substitution effect may well dominate the income effect of interest rate changes.

Finally, the last two simulations are given in Figures 7.15 and 7.16. These relate to the effects on the portfolio behaviour of the firms. Because of wide differences in the scales, we report absolute changes rather than changes in the ratios. We can make a number of observations from Figure 7.15. First, the amount of zloty time deposits held increases, as we should expect. Second, the amounts of zloty and foreign currency demand deposits also increase, but not before an immediate decline. Third, throughout the entire period of simulation, substitution takes place at the expense of foreign currency time deposits. In some ways this result parallels that for the households. The effect on the capital stock in Figure 7.16 shows that for about six months the effect is positive and increasing, then it begins to decline and after about a year it becomes negative. Needless to say, this reflects the behaviour of investment.

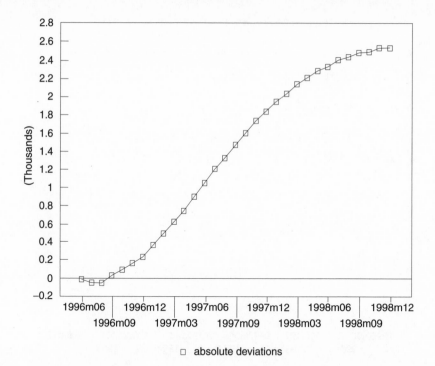

□ absolute deviations

Figure 7.14 Increase in the zloty time deposit rate (25%): effect on household consumption

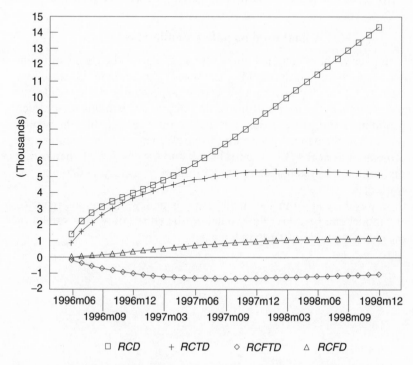

□ RCD   + RCTD   ◇ RCFTD   △ RCFD

Figure 7.15 Increase in the zloty time deposit rate (25%): absolute effects on the firm portfolio

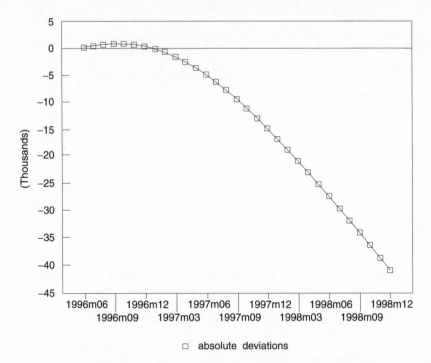

□ absolute deviations

Figure 7.16 Increase in the zloty time deposit rate (25%): effect on capital stock

A final word on policy simulations

In this chapter we have confined ourselves to simulating the effects of financial policies pertaining to the banking sector only. And even in this sector, we have been selective, emphasizing only certain aspects and leaving aside, for example, reforms in the restructuring of the commercial banking sector, such as consolidation and privatization and institutional changes like the regulatory system and the deposit insurance system. We have chosen to emphasize only those aspects of the Polish central bank and the commercial banks that are commonly and systematically used to affect monetary policy and the money market.

It is, however, clear from the small array of policy simulations reported that our model can be useful for simulating the effects of a wide variety of policies, including those other than financial.

8

SUMMARY AND CONCLUSIONS

This book is an attempt to model the Polish economy so that we can analyse some of the effects of some of the financial reforms introduced since 1990. While there is a great deal of interest in this area and there is some work which purports to study this question, the fact is that there is no full-scale study which looks at the impact of many of the reforms in any kind of a unified framework. We have tried to fill this gap to some extent. The basic approach of this study and its major findings can be summarized as follows.

As far as our approach is concerned, its distinctive features can be summarized under three headings. These are: the model, the data and the estimates. With regard to the model, our exercise clearly suggests that the proposed general equilibrium approach is a good way to model the transition economies for the purpose of analyzing the effects of financial policies. This approach allows us to take into account the specific features of these economies. For example, it allows us to take account of the special roles that foreign assets play in different sectors, foreign currency-denominated assets play in the case of the households, bank borrowings play in the case of the central government, liquidity constraints in the case of firms and the households and differential required reserve ratios for the conduct of monetary policy by the central bank. This approach also allows us to model the interaction between the behaviour of the various sectors in a reasonably detailed fashion. The upshot of the approach then is that, instead of the piecemeal treatment of the effect of any given financial policy, we have a fairly elaborate set of mechanisms through which financial policies may affect the real and the nominal variables. While the usual practice is to debate the relative importance of demand and supply side effects of such policies separately, our approach makes no such distinction. Rather, we argue that effects from both sides operate simultaneously, thus reinforcing each other. The model also enables us to take account of the less than fully developed nature of the money and capital markets in transition economies. In short, then, our approach offers a suitable framework, particularly given the limitations of the data, to examine the role of various financial reforms in Poland and the other transition economies.

An important and frustrating part of this study is the very limited amount of the data which are available, both in terms of their coverage, their length and their quality. As mentioned earlier, the time series data that are of any use date back only to 1990 or so, so that any kind of statistical analysis using annual data is virtually impossible. The use of quarterly data does not take us very far either. Thus, the only option is to work with monthly data. Here the problems are enormous, because we have monthly observations only on some of the financial variables, but not on the real variables. As a consequence we had to generate many of the series. The details of the procedures used and the actual data are described in the Appendix. There is really no way to tell what sorts of measurement errors might have crept into the generated series. Because of the generated nature of many of the series, we have not made any corrections for seasonality. Instead, we have relied on the plausibility of the estimates as judged by our *a priori* expectations about the signs and the significance of the estimated coefficients and the usual statistical criteria as well as by the within-sample forecasting ability of the model, both sectoral and for the whole economy. An advantage of using monthly data, notwithstanding the shortcomings just noted, is that it allows us to capture the role of the financial variables more realistically because many of them seem to work with shorter lags than those implied by quarterly or annual data. Anyway, our Appendix does then show that even the short annual time series data available for many of the transition economies can be used to build and estimate reasonably sized macro models.

Regarding the estimates, we believe that the sequential – that is sector-by-sector approach – which we have followed is a useful one, for it allows us to examine issues which are hard to disentangle in the complete model as well as allows us to judge the suitability and the "fit" of the individual sector models. It is most unlikely that the whole model would "behave" if the sectoral models were ill-behaved. The policy implications of the sectoral results are also interesting. If nothing else, they offer a substantial improvement over the single equation approach. But above all, because the sectoral models are based on the portfolio approach, they lend themselves to precise interpretations and analysis.

As for the major findings, they are essentially evident in Chapter 7. But to recapitulate the more controversial findings, they relate to the use of the required reserve ratio by the NBP and the role of default rates in the determination of the effective loan rate by the commercial banks. The use of the required reserve ratios by the NBP has been very vigorous and is more akin to the practices in the developing countries than in the developed countries. The high levels, as well as the frequency with which they have been used, are not found commonly in any of the developed monetary systems. Our results clearly suggest that its use of this instrument has seriously affected the liquidity and thus the loanable funds base of the commercial banks, which may have accentuated the problem of liquidity constraints in the Polish economy, thus affecting adversely both the demand and the supply sides. It is difficult to believe that this would be an intended goal of the NBP. Consequently, a serious policy implication of our results is that the NBP needs to have a closer look at its use of this instrument and to examine the rationale for not bringing these ratios and their usage more into line with those prevailing in the developed countries.

The results regarding the role of gross loan rates and loan default rates in affecting effective loan rates is another interesting finding. The issue of the loan default rates is rarely discussed in the context that we have. Our results suggest that the default rate may be used as if it were an instrument of policy by the commercial banks and, in fact, indirectly by the central bank, assuming that one of the goals of the central bank policy is to ensure adequate supply of credit at reasonable rates to the households and the firms. Our finding that a reduction in the default rate can increase the supply of loans and reduce their cost to the borrowers simultaneously shows the importance of this variable being used as an instrument of policy. The obvious question is how to achieve a given reduction and what should be the extent of the reduction. Here, obviously one has to consider the cost of actions which can lead to such reductions, such as the cost of training loan officers and the benefits in terms of increased profits for the banks and increased availability of loans to the private sector at lower rates. These kinds of calculations will clearly require a cost–benefit type of analysis. However, our results suggest that such an analysis will be well worth it.

We have frequently mentioned the importance of foreign currency holdings by the private sector in Poland, essentially as an inflation hedge. It is evident, though, that as the NBP succeeds in bringing inflation under control, the amount of such holdings will decrease. Our results show that these holdings have significant effects on the conduct of monetary policy which suggest that the NBP needs to examine the implications of the changing portfolios of the households and the firms in this respect for the use of its various instruments of monetary policy.

APPENDIX
The data set

The complete data set used to estimate and to simulate the model can be derived from this Appendix. Data series, such as changes in stocks, "real" values etc., which are used in the estimates, but which can be easily derived from the data presented below, if the remarks made below the tables are taken into account, are not presented for reasons of space.

Most data are obtained or derived from different issues of the Information Bulletins of the Narowdy Bank Polski (henceforth: **Information Bulletin**), the PlanEcon Reports (henceforth: **PlanEcon**) and the Statistical Bulletins of the Central Statistical Office (Biuletyn Statystyczny, Glowny Urzad Statystyczny, Warszawa (henceforth: **Statistical Bulletin**).

Table A1 Determination of wealth to be distributed by commercial banks

Year (Month)	CBNW	ZDNS	FCDNS	REQRES	CBNOA
1991(12)	233025	139835.8	57385.4	29229.9	−65033.7
1992(1)	246265.5	147178.2	59752.3	30578	−69913
1992(2)	255937	149605.5	67852.7	31714.8	−70193.6
1992(3)	271024.9	159089.4	69348.5	30901.8	−73488.8
1992(4)	274913.6	164250.8	69649.1	32697.9	−73711.6
1992(5)	281462.5	168434	71806.8	29938.2	−71159.9
1992(6)	297166.6	178083.4	71943.6	30660	−77799.6
1992(7)	307204.2	187215	74291	31626.2	−77324.4
1992(8)	313244.5	192960.5	75560.7	33163	−77886.3
1992(9)	326043.8	199545.5	79011.6	32101.6	−79588.3
1992(10)	335574.4	207412.2	83424.3	33035.4	−77773.3
1992(11)	339939.1	213029.9	87339.9	33772.6	−73341.9
1992(12)	380654.8	230492.8	90872.7	34878.1	−94167.4
1993(1)	382846.9	234231.7	92627.2	38620.1	−94608.1
1993(2)	392549.6	237014.5	95436.8	37892.6	−97990.9
1993(3)	405725.2	243859.7	98186.1	37554.6	−101234
1993(4)	415661.7	246351.1	99775.4	38855.5	−108391
1993(5)	422956.1	250717.2	102593.9	39101.2	−108746
1993(6)	432158.3	252004	107416.4	40183.5	−112921
1993(7)	440192.1	259619.7	112963.3	40235.7	−107845
1993(8)	465083.6	265238.4	125935.5	41653.3	−115563
1993(9)	491721.5	266083.5	127950.5	42712.4	−140400
1993(10)	497529	271346.3	133343.7	43140.4	−135979
1993(11)	535289.7	276707.6	152222.9	43951.8	−150311
1993(12)	536213.4	298413.3	160805.6	46732	−123727
1994(1)	542763.6	296755.6	163764.5	49837.2	−132081
1994(2)	562419	303924.2	167788.3	50101	−140808
1994(3)	566932.2	306184.9	169941.1	51244.2	−142050
1994(4)	575606.2	309614.4	171738.2	51089.7	−145343
1994(5)	599678.4	318808.8	175110.8	51149.4	−156908
1994(6)	617649.6	328283	180430	53682.4	−162619
1994(7)	634628	342321	186902	54463	−159868
1994(8)	644080	357121	192543	56126	−150542
1994(9)	672354	363488	196574	59466	−171758
1994(10)	687908	367006	200738	63323	−183487
1994(11)	742145	380016	209605	56973	−209497
1994(12)	755044	429687	220511	56968	−161814
1995(1)	763915	412117	222760	62707	−191745
1995(2)	783256	424479	221643	63055	−200189
1995(3)	816770	447556	220626	61516	−210104
1995(4)	835447	464162	217935	61494	−214844
1995(5)	851314	487155	206177	65209	−223191
1995(6)	861364	500083	206646	69740	−224375
1995(7)	884928	524759	208242	71148	−223075
1995(8)	892994	549083	210336	73418	−206993
1995(9)	901034	557869	207745	73413	−208833
1995(10)	920905	580913	208437	77971	−209526
1995(11)	948371	595800	209399	80424	−223596
1995(12)	975096	634212	212998	80418	−208304

Table A1 – cont.

Year (Month)	CBNW	ZDNS	FCDNS	REQRES	CBNOA
1996(1)	978600	646626	214514	86401	−203861
1996(2)	994725	665795	212881	91328	−207377
1996(3)	985761	688642	211272	91320	−177167
1996(4)	993875	703960	213410	95733	−172238
1996(5)	1024870	719715	214723	97444	−187876

CBNW = nominal wealth to be distributed by commercial banks; calculated as zloty deposits of the non-financial sector (*ZDNS*), plus foreign currency deposits of non-financial sector (*FCDNS*) – both from the liability side of Table 2, **Information Bulletin** – minus required reserves (*REQRES*: Table 1, **Information Bulletin**: required reserves held), minus net other assets (*CBNOA*). Net other assets is the difference between all assets and liabilities given in Table 2 of the **Information Bulletins**, but which are not explicitly distinguished in our model. This mainly refers to the balance of the items "Other Assets" and "Other Liabilities," which, e.g. include fixed assets, accrued receivables, capital, net interbank settlements and the allowance for loan losses. Note that this implies that $CBNW = L_f + GOV + CBNFA + ER - CBL$ (see below). In the simulation model, and in the estimates, we have used "real" values of the stocks, and changes in "real" values. The real stocks (*RCBNW, RZDNS, RFCDNS, RREQRES* and *RCBNOA*, respectively) are found by deflating the nominal stocks by the consumer price index. Real flows are derived from the real stocks.

Table A2 Distribution of wealth of commercial banks

Year (Month)	CBL	L_f	GOV	CBNFA	ER
1991(12)	72549.1	186280.5	60070.7	40820.2	18402.7
1992(1)	76762.1	189054.2	67742.4	47099.4	19131.6
1992(2)	75179.8	192797.1	77450	49745.3	11124.4
1992(3)	77468.5	200676.8	81617.5	50611.7	15587.4
1992(4)	80246.2	202415.5	84968.4	54081.3	13694.6
1992(5)	78516.1	202098.8	89961.3	55061.5	12857
1992(6)	76666.8	211559	88015.3	57892.8	16366.3
1992(7)	77723.8	214818.8	96155.5	60498.9	13454.8
1992(8)	77947.3	219139.1	99250.4	60312.9	12489.4
1992(9)	78732.4	220550.5	103458.8	65262.2	15504.7
1992(10)	83077.5	224808.7	107664.3	70514.7	15664.2
1992(11)	86587.9	224109.5	112643.6	72683.3	17090.6
1992(12)	47985.4	236770	93735.4	74537.2	23597.6
1993(1)	47991.5	239043.1	98448.5	81035.6	12311.2
1993(2)	48635.1	243570.1	107044.3	81303.3	9267
1993(3)	49103.1	252396.4	109901.5	81921.3	10609.1
1993(4)	49992.4	257667.2	108126.7	87301.6	12558.6
1993(5)	48280.9	260653.9	110536.2	86219.5	13827.4
1993(6)	54336.3	269421.7	115282.7	88380.9	13409.3
1993(7)	51245.3	274496	115697.5	91086.7	10157.2
1993(8)	51946.6	281788	127565	96273.3	11403.9
1993(9)	52304.2	288714.3	147740.6	97143	10427.8
1993(10)	55301.3	296092.5	146478.5	102013.1	8246.2
1993(11)	55956.1	301695.2	164804.6	109213.4	15532.6
1993(12)	62656.9	309304.8	173376.8	95103	21085.7
1994(1)	63452.4	316747.6	176511.1	101039.1	11918.2
1994(2)	64298	322138.1	181354.9	107224.2	15999.8
1994(3)	66202.1	328817.7	184421.5	109015.3	10879.8
1994(4)	64702.8	333251.3	183158.1	112362.1	11537.5
1994(5)	63839.7	335729.6	189510	115382.8	22895.7
1994(6)	64777.2	343814	201893.5	120830.2	15889.1
1994(7)	65064	348505	210509	127177	13501
1994(8)	63846	350457	218248	132757	6464
1994(9)	64328	356990	225422	135871	18399
1994(10)	66392	365737	227030	143478	18055
1994(11)	68354	377451	257327	143185	32536
1994(12)	70277	382144	265166	151082	26929
1995(1)	69998	391461	265058	157578	19816
1995(2)	69039	396905	273081	157757	24552
1995(3)	68881	411968	283319	149740	40624
1995(4)	69814	419751	303128	148922	33460
1995(5)	69470	424872	311366	137779	46767
1995(6)	69639	437871	322414	136929	33789
1995(7)	72011	448916	319227	134788	54008
1995(8)	74213	459005	328181	130517	49504
1995(9)	72878	471947	329927	124571	47467
1995(10)	74772	485626	334832	124062	51157
1995(11)	75825	502079	347387	120783	53947
1995(12)	77739	505892	376087	125489	45367

Table A2 – cont.

Year (Month)	CBL	L_f	GOV	CBNFA	ER
1996(1)	77436	512004	375620	117171	51241
1996(2)	77080	523762	376170	108616	63257
1996(3)	74505	531540	372985	106018	49723
1996(4)	84056	539879	391187	101184	45681
1996(5)	84608	544451	400570	101709	62748

CBL = commercial banks' liabilities to the central bank (approximated by DUE to financial institutions, NBP, on liability side of Table 2, **Information Bulletin**).

L_f = nominal loans to firms (from the asset side; Table 2, **Information Bulletin**: due from non-financial sector, corporate).

GOV = nominal loans to government (calculated as the sum of the treasury bills and the treasury bonds [long term], both from asset side of Table 2, **Information Bulletin**). In fact, *GOV* refers to government bonds purchased by the commercial banks. Due to its relative unimportance loans from commercial bank loans to the government (in **Information Bulletin**: due from general government) are not considered.

CBNFA = net foreign assets (from the asset and liability side of Table 2, **Information Bulletin**: calculated as due from abroad minus foreign liabilities).

ER = excess reserves (free reserves). Calculated as total reserves minus required reserves. Total reserves are approximated on the asset side of Table 2: due from financial institutions, vault cash plus NBP, from the **Information Bulletin**.

Table A3 Determination of the real disposable income of households

Year (Month)	Y	TR	HTAX	H	W
1991(12)	—	15054.2	—	16588748	—
1992(1)	50629.43	15203.1	730	16067539	0.002487
1992(2)	46870.96	15277.4	3610	15864077	0.002497
1992(3)	48342	15734.6	5528	16100955	0.002717
1992(4)	49190.01	17507.8	5818	15965207	0.002833
1992(5)	46330.27	18122.2	5363	15890099	0.002708
1992(6)	46138	18328.3	6233	15931078	0.002786
1992(7)	48111.09	18289.6	5715	15980976	0.002946
1992(8)	45989.5	18426.8	7130	15879467	0.002978
1992(9)	45340.54	18826.7	7653	15872824	0.003127
1992(10)	46326.72	18822.4	7393	15873070	0.003311
1992(11)	47679.58	18958.4	8127	15955085	0.003541
1992(12)	52275.69	22664.9	8934	15941435	0.003871
1993(1)	45544.15	22694.5	7204	15873143	0.003334
1993(2)	45328.2	22705.5	8132	15610111	0.003575
1993(3)	48717.47	23850.8	8810	15745050	0.003952
1993(4)	47290.67	24232.1	9384	15708194	0.003938
1993(5)	44651.76	24102.6	10662	15725650	0.003837
1993(6)	46006.7	24113.6	8312	15553605	0.003935
1993(7)	44919.53	24159.5	10051	15446642	0.004009
1993(8)	44383.45	24153.7	10590	15544426	0.004072
1993(9)	44525.58	24237.5	10269	15546623	0.004185
1993(10)	44349.91	24515.1	11561	15550477	0.004324
1993(11)	45084.29	24632.7	11694	15516381	0.004634
1993(12)	49172.7	27649.7	12755	15515496	0.005333
1994(1)	44490.29	28418.5	10600	15535275	0.004642
1994(2)	44090.02	28363	11377	15491796	0.004718
1994(3)	49758.15	31577.1	11795	15494325	0.005419
1994(4)	46973.82	32338.4	14148	15515496	0.00532
1994(5)	44021.82	32022.5	14282	14703796	0.005327
1994(6)	46911.8	35380.1	12319	14735675	0.00554
1994(7)	45389.33	35942.5	15120	14662970	0.005593
1994(8)	44250.16	35591.7	15541	14685790	0.005575
1994(9)	43886.05	35968.9	16080	14755209	0.005816
1994(10)	43848.09	36054.1	16470	14719315	0.006051
1994(11)	46070.19	36347.7	17610	14750766	0.006612
1994(12)	51245.07	39543.3	18420	14899500	0.007426
1995(1)	44648.05	40309	15760	14872431	0.006385
1995(2)	44087.67	40320	16980	15093116	0.006438
1995(3)	49257.88	44660	14860	15128018	0.007072
1995(4)	48006.8	44680	18810	15122883	0.007309
1995(5)	46600.45	44549	19860	15083593	0.0073
1995(6)	47361.43	44797	17350	15147060	0.007321
1995(7)	46942.07	44874	19970	15062207	0.007362
1995(8)	47393.73	45138	20520	15007368	0.007527
1995(9)	47102.25	45455	20460	15057467	0.007695
1995(10)	47782.55	45929	21760	15066185	0.008043
1995(11)	49768.62	46188	22950	15071407	0.00863
1995(12)	52713.99	51638	25840	15014153	0.00926

Table A3 – cont.

Year (Month)	Y	TR	HTAX	H	W
1996(1)	49329.36	52929	17850	14931900	0.00829
1996(2)	48025.22	52508	20180	14904710	0.00841
1996(3)	50878.09	52750	15590	14975299	0.008843
1996(4)	51038.19	54011	18080	15014930	0.009181
1996(5)	50113.24	54057	20740	14900807	0.009363

Y: real *disposable* income. Calculated by deflating nominal disposable income with the consumer price index. Nominal disposable income is calculated as the sum of nominal labour income (*LABINC*: see Table A14 below) plus nominal transfers to households (*TR*), minus nominal direct taxes for households (*HTAX*). Nominal labour income is calculated by multiplying total employment (*H*) with the (nominal) gross wage rate (*W*).

TR: transfers to households. Taken from the **Statistical Bulletin**, Table 14, the column grant total of gross social benefits.

HTAX: direct taxes for households (personal income taxes). Taken from different issues of the **PlanEcon**. These figures are also given in **Statistical Bulletins** (Table 17).

H: employment. Approximated by using the unemployment rate (*UNR*) and figures for unemployment (*UNEMPL*: see Table A4). The formula used is: $H = (UNEMPL/UNR) - UNEMPL$.

W: nominal wage rate. Approximated by the row gross average monthly wages and salaries of the corporate sector, as given in the **Information Bulletin** (Table 1).

Table A4 Population, unemployment and labour share

Year (Month)	POP	LABF	UNR	UNEMPL	LABSHARE
1991(12)	38309000	18744348	11.5	2155600	—
1992(1)	38318000	18279339	12.1	2211800	0.685669
1992(2)	38323000	18109677	12.4	2245600	0.69103
1992(3)	38333000	18317355	12.1	2216400	0.675272
1992(4)	38343000	18183607	12.2	2218400	0.644823
1992(5)	38353000	18118699	12.3	2228600	0.665365
1992(6)	38365000	18227778	12.6	2296700	0.642278
1992(7)	38379000	18390076	13.1	2409100	0.68418
1992(8)	38389000	18336567	13.4	2457100	0.678158
1992(9)	38401000	18371324	13.6	2498500	0.71409
1992(10)	38408000	18350370	13.5	2477300	0.641633
1992(11)	38413000	18445185	13.5	2490100	0.774898
1992(12)	38418000	18450735	13.6	2509300	0.637365
1993(1)	38421000	18457143	14	2584000	0.709454
1993(2)	38426000	18236111	14.4	2626000	0.749209
1993(3)	38432000	18393750	14.4	2648700	0.69822
1993(4)	38439000	18350694	14.4	2642500	0.691446
1993(5)	38449000	18349650	14.3	2624000	0.655971
1993(6)	38459000	18255405	14.8	2701800	0.600466
1993(7)	38471000	18258442	15.4	2811800	0.638028
1993(8)	38482000	18374026	15.4	2829600	0.638969
1993(9)	38491000	18376623	15.4	2830000	0.668494
1993(10)	38498000	18359477	15.3	2809000	0.588968
1993(11)	38501000	18362581	15.5	2846200	0.663213
1993(12)	38505000	18405096	15.7	2889600	0.679211
1994(1)	38508000	18494375	16	2959100	0.859698
1994(2)	38512000	18464596	16.1	2972800	0.784033
1994(3)	38521000	18445625	16	2951300	0.783199
1994(4)	38528000	18405096	15.7	2889600	0.755909
1994(5)	38537000	17546296	16.2	2842500	0.694301
1994(6)	38544000	17668675	16.6	2933000	0.696798
1994(7)	38552000	17644970	16.9	2982000	0.63896
1994(8)	38558000	17651190	16.8	2965400	0.615304
1994(9)	38566000	17670909	16.5	2915700	0.659189
1994(10)	38568000	17564815	16.2	2845500	0.632385
1994(11)	38572000	17581366	16.1	2830600	0.713445
1994(12)	38581000	17737500	16	2838000	0.682893
1995(1)	38573000	17747531	16.2	2875100	0.826552
1995(2)	38575000	17925316	15.8	2832200	0.799487
1995(3)	38578000	17881818	15.4	2753800	0.739978
1995(4)	38578000	17812583	15.1	2689700	0.798901
1995(5)	38581000	17682993	14.7	2599400	0.760198
1995(6)	38587000	17841060	15.1	2694000	0.735931
1995(7)	38595000	17783007	15.3	2720800	0.748612
1995(8)	38604000	17697368	15.2	2690000	0.728328
1995(9)	38609000	17714667	15	2657200	0.755275
1995(10)	38613000	17662585	14.7	2596400	0.72164
1995(11)	38614000	17668707	14.7	2597300	0.805345
1995(12)	38609000	17642953	14.9	2628800	0.732705

Table A4 – cont.

Year (Month)	POP	LABF	UNR	UNEMPL	LABSHARE
1996(1)	38601000	17650000	15.4	2718100	0.876125
1996(2)	38600000	17638710	15.5	2734000	0.786937
1996(3)	38602000	17701299	15.4	2726000	0.729514
1996(4)	38606000	17685430	15.1	2670500	0.779147
1996(5)	38612000	17468707	14.7	2567900	0.756488

POP: population, given by **Statistical Bulletins** (Table 4).
LABF: calculated as *UNEMP/UNR*.
UNR: unemployment rate (%), given in Table 1 of **Information Bulletins**.
UNEMPL: unemployed, taken from Table 1 of **Information Bulletins**.
LABSHARE: calculated as real labour income (*RLABINC*, see Table A14 for nominal labour income) over real GDP (*RGDP*: see Table A16 below). The average labour share is used as a coefficient in the Cobb–Douglas production function.

Table A5 Assets of households

Year (Month)	HFD	HFTD	HD	HTD	CUR=CUR$_s$
1991(12)	17172.9	37045.6	4193.5	64389.1	68282.6
1992(1)	17616.7	38970.8	4377.1	69412	68589
1992(2)	19480.7	44812.1	4346.1	74637	71089.5
1992(3)	19345.6	46334.2	4691.4	78833.1	71199.9
1992(4)	18651.2	47683.1	4982.9	81433.8	75351.6
1992(5)	19727	48593	5115.7	84097.5	75604.1
1992(6)	19748.6	48684.6	5363	87816.3	78547.8
1992(7)	20377	50311.9	5785.7	91609.7	82735.5
1992(8)	20772.4	51162	6028	94946.3	84282
1992(9)	21747.8	53677.3	6325.3	99097.3	85721.3
1992(10)	22592	57344.4	6378.6	103363.5	89158.4
1992(11)	23354.7	60244.2	6426.8	106661.4	91656
1992(12)	24641.2	62682.2	7178.4	114501.4	95245.6
1993(1)	24635.5	64365.8	7300.6	122360.2	93592.3
1993(2)	24721.8	66911.7	7457.1	129445.4	96016.5
1993(3)	25022.6	68864.3	8268.1	133983.9	100558.7
1993(4)	25587.6	69994.6	8588.8	135725.8	105516.3
1993(5)	26234.4	71857	8948.7	136077.4	106013.1
1993(6)	27220.6	75325	9094.8	136683.6	108895.1
1993(7)	29546.1	78240.3	9704	139450.1	109722
1993(8)	33501.7	86229.8	10309.3	140946.3	112042.5
1993(9)	34685.8	87741	10478.7	142472.8	112245.4
1993(10)	36739.1	91237.2	11219.2	143578.4	117860
1993(11)	41227.4	105541.2	11612.4	143576.1	120218.9
1993(12)	45405.5	108866.4	14061.7	148593.3	121830
1994(1)	45431.3	111291	16124.6	150117	120736.9
1994(2)	46593.4	113343.1	15400.6	152296	125354.7
1994(3)	48103.1	114180.2	17221.1	154380.5	133351.2
1994(4)	48103.1	116280	17826.1	158248.7	137054.3
1994(5)	49228.5	118128.7	17830.2	162518.1	136961.9
1994(6)	52195	119661	18021	167600	142289.2
1994(7)	54975	122482	19997	172570	148175
1994(8)	57337	125954	19367	176691	149116
1994(9)	58884	128205	19555	180067	147384
1994(10)	61225	130216	19601	183666	149593
1994(11)	65021	135263	21061	187517	149494
1994(12)	70354	138710	22896	198099	147800
1995(1)	70119	141124	23443	211820	149301
1995(2)	68987	141210	25604	224308	157773
1995(3)	68407	140713	27360	240435	164957
1995(4)	67081	139241	30264	254240	181492
1995(5)	64008	132203	31522	264780	180341
1995(6)	64800	132454	31962	274740	189177
1995(7)	65898	132441	33535	288500	195961
1995(8)	66901	134033	35267	301352	198797
1995(9)	66154	131682	36072	311645	201411
1995(10)	66751	131420	37839	323464	209744
1995(11)	67714	131998	40575	335868	215421
1995(12)	68597	128525	44707	352019	224099

Table A5 – cont.

Year (Month)	HFD	HFTD	HD	HTD	CUR=CUR$_s$
1996(1)	67897	129364	48932	374387	219008
1996(2)	66722	127957	54915	390498	225472
1996(3)	65969	126255	59522	403585	230679
1996(4)	66382	126038	64242	413904	245212
1996(5)	66952	125819	66782	421833	243188

HFD: foreign currency-denominated demand deposits held by households. Taken from Table 2, **Information Bulletin**.

HFTD: foreign currency-denominated time deposits held by households. Taken from Table 2, **Information Bulletin**.

HD: zloty demand deposits held by households. Taken from Table 2, **Information Bulletin**.

HTD: zloty time deposits held by households. Taken from Table 2, **Information Bulletin**. Here time deposits personal plus savings account is used.

CUR = CUR$_s$: currency (supply and demand). Approximated by notes and coin in circulation. Taken from Table 3, **Information Bulletin**.

Note that in the table above all variables are in current prices, whereas the estimates are done on "real" variables, which are obtained by deflating the nominal stocks with the consumer price index.

Table A6 Net foreign assets, net other assets and net wealth of households

Year (Month)	US$FDEBT	US$CURAC	HNFA	RHNOA	RHNW
1991(12)	48400	−218	346465.1	0	537548.8
1992(1)	48400	−89	340699.2	47969.73	549983.5
1992(2)	46300	−67	304092.9	89210.53	563121.2
1992(3)	45500	289	292272.8	115924	575312
1992(4)	45400	176	286842.1	139750.7	584819.6
1992(5)	46000	31	293806.1	159258.7	596919.4
1992(6)	48200	49	318980.3	152423.1	609237.3
1992(7)	49300	49	327782.3	152739	619353.6
1992(8)	50900	42	346160.7	154484.1	628072.3
1992(9)	50300	−201	333759	191334	639005.9
1992(10)	47800	−64	291291	235351.8	648188.8
1992(11)	46900	−260	273714.9	263782.4	661840.5
1992(12)	47000	−224	270860	275239.9	673790.7
1993(1)	47700	−244	278300.9	289049.5	682186.2
1993(2)	46800	−128	260957	317394.3	694493.2
1993(3)	47500	−291	270624	322582.2	705543.3
1993(4)	48800	−163	284401.1	326651.3	714962.4
1993(5)	48800	−361	277735.4	342431.2	721836
1993(6)	47400	−445	244804.2	367504.1	727161.4
1993(7)	47200	−169	233578	376470.7	731088.8
1993(8)	47600	−115	229445.4	383312	737016.7
1993(9)	48400	−414	232025.5	395208.1	744327.8
1993(10)	47300	47	202389	415400.2	748916
1993(11)	46800	16	186393.1	433819.6	757239
1993(12)	47200	−62	200728.6	446957.8	769024.6
1994(1)	47400	−191	192908.8	466465.4	781414.7
1994(2)	47600	84	189135.8	479393.2	793674.5
1994(3)	48200	−331	187317.8	492366.7	806324.6
1994(4)	45000	45	111725.4	541804	816582
1994(5)	45500	−30	119782.4	547515	824513.8
1994(6)	46800	−104	145266.2	546311.3	835333
1994(7)	47200	350	145233.7	548890.1	841727.5
1994(8)	47000	−18	123254	562699	845654.2
1994(9)	47500	−369	124256.7	578185.2	851531
1994(10)	49100	−58	176866.9	566763.2	857792.7
1994(11)	41300	−124	−36148.6	660824	867748.9
1994(12)	42200	−198	−26584.2	664339	878733.5
1995(1)	42500	−129	−34698.2	681112.7	890737.1
1995(2)	43400	−81	−33907.1	689422.9	903074.6
1995(3)	44100	−395	−32472.6	697298	916742
1995(4)	44900	−2	−46753.6	711593.2	931761.7
1995(5)	44700	−5	−55951	731248.4	944508.7
1995(6)	44500	−183	−81092	748254.4	957785.1
1995(7)	45000	−108	−97851	756447.8	970254.5
1995(8)	43800	−198	−156018	781897.7	981804.8
1995(9)	44200	−281	−172368	802783.1	994927.9
1995(10)	44300	−591	−196510	820039.9	1008316
1995(11)	43900	−156	−231543	843294.8	1025098
1995(12)	43900	28	−236964	856116.3	1041929

Table A6 – *cont.*

Year (Month)	US$FDEBT	US$CURAC	HNFA	RHNOA	RHNW
1996(1)	43100	−162	−276690	880619.8	1055405
1996(2)	43400	169	−285476	890345.8	1067038
1996(3)	43100	144	−298736	902141.1	1078337
1996(4)	42700	−377	−320353	915424.9	1090293
1996(5)	42565	19	−344941	932749.9	1100819

US$FDEBT: gross hard currency debt (in million US$). Taken from **PlanEcon**.
US$CURAC: current account balance (in million US$). Taken from **PlanEcon**.
HNFA: nominal stock of net foreign assets held by households. It is calculated as $HNFA_{-1} +$ $\Delta HNFA$. $\Delta HNFA$ is calculated as $(\Delta US\$FDEBT + \Delta US\$CURAC + US\$\Delta FDI)EXCHR/1000 -$ $\Delta CBNFA - \Delta FRES$. $US\$\Delta FDI$ is the foreign direct investment in US dollars (see for foreign direct investment in zloty Table A12 below). *EXCHR* is the exchange rate (see Table A9 below). *CBNFA*, see Table A2. $\Delta FRES$ is the change in net foreign asset holdings of the central bank (international reserves: see Table A17 below). The starting value of HNFA is set at 346465.1. In the model we have used RHNFA, which is HNFA deflated by the consumer price index. $\Delta RHNFA$ is $RHNFA - RHNFA_{-1}$. See also the explanation in Chapter 4.
RHNOA: real stock of net other assets held by households. It is determined as $RHNOA_{-1} +$ $\Delta RHNOA$. $\Delta RHNOA$ is determined via the budget constraint of households (see equation **6.16** in Chapter 6, p. 90). Starting value for *RHNOA* is set at zero.
RHNW: real net wealth of households. It is calculated as the sum of all real assets held by households.

Table A7 Yield indicators

Year (Month)	IG	ICB	IE	IF
1991(12)	0.017882	0.027616	0.003651	0.028436
1992(1)	0.030555	0.027616	0.003314	0.028436
1992(2)	0.031032	0.027616	0.00333	0.028436
1992(3)	0.031803	0.027616	0.003474	0.028436
1992(4)	0.031921	0.027616	0.003274	0.028436
1992(5)	0.031744	0.027616	0.003129	0.028436
1992(6)	0.032215	0.02741	0.003161	0.028436
1992(7)	0.028864	0.025745	0.002766	0.027204
1992(8)	0.028742	0.025745	0.002717	0.027204
1992(9)	0.02862	0.025745	0.002572	0.027204
1992(10)	0.027822	0.025745	0.002677	0.027204
1992(11)	0.02564	0.025745	0.002935	0.027204
1992(12)	0.026706	0.025745	0.002855	0.027822
1993(1)	0.025923	0.025745	0.00262	0.027822
1993(2)	0.022751	0.023621	0.002564	0.027822
1993(3)	0.019392	0.023621	0.002555	0.025324
1993(4)	0.021355	0.023621	0.002539	0.025324
1993(5)	0.022868	0.023621	0.002547	0.025324
1993(6)	0.023082	0.023621	0.002636	0.025324
1993(7)	0.023173	0.023621	0.002596	0.025324
1993(8)	0.023179	0.023621	0.00258	0.025324
1993(9)	0.023296	0.023621	0.002564	0.025324
1993(10)	0.022842	0.023621	0.002661	0.025324
1993(11)	0.022777	0.023621	0.00275	0.025324
1993(12)	0.022887	0.023621	0.002677	0.025324
1994(1)	0.02266	0.023621	0.002588	0.025324
1994(2)	0.020578	0.023621	0.002814	0.025324
1994(3)	0.020432	0.023621	0.003089	0.025324
1994(4)	0.020858	0.023621	0.003282	0.025324
1994(5)	0.020578	0.02254	0.003683	0.02405
1994(6)	0.020205	0.02254	0.003691	0.023406
1994(7)	0.020205	0.02254	0.003859	0.022757
1994(8)	0.020118	0.02254	0.003923	0.022757
1994(9)	0.020011	0.02254	0.004098	0.022757
1994(10)	0.020011	0.02254	0.00448	0.022757
1994(11)	0.020078	0.02254	0.004702	0.022757
1994(12)	0.020024	0.02254	0.005096	0.022757
1995(1)	0.019917	0.02254	0.005057	0.020785
1995(2)	0.020071	0.024263	0.004994	0.020785
1995(3)	0.020891	0.024263	0.004986	0.020785
1995(4)	0.020418	0.024263	0.004954	0.020785
1995(5)	0.018783	0.021667	0.004883	0.020785
1995(6)	0.018681	0.021667	0.004789	0.019446
1995(7)	0.018742	0.021667	0.004686	0.019446
1995(8)	0.018729	0.021667	0.004686	0.019446
1995(9)	0.018593	0.020341	0.004654	0.018088
1995(10)	0.018081	0.020341	0.004702	0.018088
1995(11)	0.018088	0.020341	0.004662	0.018088
1995(12)	0.018088	0.020341	0.004567	0.018088

Table A7 – cont.

Year (Month)	IG	ICB	IE	IF
1996(1)	0.017107	0.018769	0.004384	0.017607
1996(2)	0.016117	0.018769	0.004194	0.017228
1996(3)	0.016201	0.018769	0.004305	0.017228
1996(4)	0.016284	0.018769	0.004363	0.017228
1996(5)	0.016277	0.018769	0.004311	0.016591

IG: lending rate on loans to government. Approximated by yields on bills purchased, 8-week bills: Table 1, **Information Bulletin**.

ICB: lending rate on commercial bank lending from central bank. Approximated by the average of refinancing credit interest rate, the Lombard credit interest rate and the rediscount credit interest rate, see Table 1, **Information Bulletin**.

IE: foreign interest rate. Approximated by US deposit rate, taken from **International Financial Statistics**, IMF.

IF: loan rate for firms. Approximated by: interest rates on credits in main commercial banks, on credit with lowest risk rates, **Information Bulletin**, Table 1.

It should be noted that we have obtained the above given interest rates by recalculating the interest rates on a yearly basis in interest rates on a monthly basis, by using the following formula: $i_e = (i_{e,y} + 1)^{(1/12)} - 1$, where $i_{e,y}$ is the corresponding interest rate on a yearly basis.

Table A8 Other yield indicators

Year (Month)	IFD	IFTD	ID	ITD
1991(12)	0.002466	0.004074	0.007207	0.025955
1992(1)	0.002466	0.004074	0.007207	0.025955
1992(2)	0.002466	0.004074	0.007207	0.025955
1992(3)	0.002466	0.003675	0.007207	0.025955
1992(4)	0.002466	0.003675	0.004472	0.025955
1992(5)	0.002466	0.003675	0.004472	0.025955
1992(6)	0.002466	0.003675	0.004472	0.025955
1992(7)	0.002466	0.003675	0.004074	0.023406
1992(8)	0.002466	0.003675	0.004074	0.023406
1992(9)	0.002466	0.003675	0.004074	0.023406
1992(10)	0.002466	0.003675	0.004074	0.023406
1992(11)	0.002466	0.003675	0.004074	0.023406
1992(12)	0.002466	0.003675	0.004074	0.023406
1993(1)	0.002466	0.002871	0.004074	0.023406
1993(2)	0.002466	0.002871	0.004074	0.023406
1993(3)	0.001652	0.002466	0.004074	0.018769
1993(4)	0.001652	0.002466	0.004074	0.018769
1993(5)	0.001652	0.002466	0.004074	0.018769
1993(6)	0.001652	0.002466	0.004074	0.018769
1993(7)	0.001652	0.00206	0.004074	0.018769
1993(8)	0.001652	0.00206	0.004074	0.018769
1993(9)	0.001652	0.00206	0.004074	0.018769
1993(10)	0.001652	0.00206	0.004074	0.018769
1993(11)	0.001652	0.002263	0.004074	0.018769
1993(12)	0.001652	0.002263	0.004074	0.018769
1994(1)	0.001652	0.002263	0.004074	0.018769
1994(2)	0.001652	0.00206	0.004074	0.018769
1994(3)	0.001652	0.00206	0.004074	0.018769
1994(4)	0.001652	0.00206	0.004074	0.018769
1994(5)	0.001652	0.00206	0.003899	0.018769
1994(6)	0.001652	0.00206	0.004074	0.018769
1994(7)	0.001856	0.002263	0.004074	0.018769
1994(8)	0.001856	0.002263	0.004074	0.019446
1994(9)	0.001856	0.002263	0.004074	0.019446
1994(10)	0.001652	0.002263	0.004074	0.019446
1994(11)	0.001652	0.002263	0.004074	0.019446
1994(12)	0.001652	0.002466	0.004074	0.019446
1995(1)	0.001652	0.002466	0.004074	0.018769
1995(2)	0.001652	0.002466	0.004074	0.018769
1995(3)	0.001652	0.002466	0.004074	0.018769
1995(4)	0.001652	0.002466	0.004074	0.018769
1995(5)	0.001652	0.002466	0.004074	0.017401
1995(6)	0.001652	0.002466	0.004868	0.016709
1995(7)	0.001652	0.002466	0.004868	0.016709
1995(8)	0.001652	0.002466	0.004868	0.016709
1995(9)	0.001652	0.002466	0.004868	0.014956
1995(10)	0.001652	0.002466	0.004868	0.014956
1995(11)	0.001652	0.002466	0.004868	0.014956
1995(12)	0.001241	0.002466	0.004868	0.014956

Table A8 – cont.

Year (Month)	IFD	IFTD	ID	ITD
1996(1)	0.001241	0.002466	0.004868	0.01353
1996(2)	0.001241	0.002263	0.004868	0.01353
1996(3)	0.001241	0.002466	0.004868	0.01353
1996(4)	0.001652	0.002304	0.004868	0.01353
1996(5)	0.001241	0.002304	0.004868	0.01353

ID: the zloty deposit rate.
ITD: the zloty time deposit rate.
IFD: the foreign currency demand deposit rate.
IFTD: the foreign currency time deposit rate.
All rates are taken from Table 1 in the **Information Bulletins** (for the time deposit rate the 6-months rate is used). The interest rates presented in the Table are recalculated interest rates on a monthly basis.

Table A9 Default rate, prices, exchange rate and household tax rate

Year (Month)	DEF	P	EXCHR	htaxr
1991(12)	0.15211	1	11564	—
1992(1)	0.16373	1.075	11387	0.018271
1992(2)	0.208465	1.094	13051	0.09114
1992(3)	0.21887	1.116	13627	0.126374
1992(4)	0.224891	1.157	13598	0.128651
1992(5)	0.228007	1.204	13805	0.124656
1992(6)	0.231757	1.224	13523	0.140454
1992(7)	0.235032	1.24	13484	0.121381
1992(8)	0.236299	1.274	13620	0.15076
1992(9)	0.237514	1.341	13823	0.154207
1992(10)	0.240313	1.381	14964	0.140691
1992(11)	0.240102	1.412	15564	0.143861
1992(12)	0.234926	1.443	15879	0.144791
1993(1)	0.241	1.502163	15726	0.136119
1993(2)	0.238	1.552668	16213	0.145719
1993(3)	0.25	1.585857	16707	0.141599
1993(4)	0.247	1.621932	16471	0.151712
1993(5)	0.2395	1.652235	16792	0.176715
1993(6)	0.233	1.67388	17713	0.135799
1993(7)	0.23	1.692639	18121	0.162312
1993(8)	0.2365	1.7316	19439	0.167323
1993(9)	0.243	1.77489	19495	0.15784
1993(10)	0.243	1.808079	20197	0.171952
1993(11)	0.2495	1.881672	20558	0.162654
1993(12)	0.256	1.985568	21308	0.154156
1994(1)	0.257	2.021308	21362	0.146997
1994(2)	0.264	2.043149	21599	0.155644
1994(3)	0.271	2.084846	21734	0.14049
1994(4)	0.259	2.144413	22088	0.171406
1994(5)	0.272	2.182139	22238	0.182352
1994(6)	0.258	2.231778	22233	0.150902
1994(7)	0.273	2.265533	22472	0.184371
1994(8)	0.274	2.303259	22789	0.189828
1994(9)	0.274	2.408494	22972	0.18739
1994(10)	0.269	2.477989	22931	0.184909
1994(11)	0.261	2.523657	24513	0.180564
1994(12)	0.252	2.571311	24261	0.16648
1995(1)	0.2435	2.676734	23977	0.165961
1995(2)	0.2435	2.733303	23959	0.174754
1995(3)	0.235	2.777015	23509	0.138892
1995(4)	0.232	2.841298	23312	0.170178
1995(5)	0.220238	2.892724	23113	0.18036
1995(6)	0.222	2.921009	23260	0.156453
1995(7)	0.215	2.892724	23457	0.180094
1995(8)	0.21	2.90301	24179	0.181647
1995(9)	0.202188	2.990434	24467	0.176591
1995(10)	0.203	3.04186	24252	0.179569
1995(11)	0.196	3.08043	24550	0.176442
1995(12)	0.189241	3.126714	24942	0.185868

Table A9 – cont.

Year (Month)	DEF	P	EXCHR	htaxr
1996(1)	0.182716	3.220515	24961	0.144199
1996(2)	0.176415	3.283049	25313	0.161001
1996(3)	0.170332	3.333077	25620	0.117731
1996(4)	0.164458	3.404991	26057	0.131154
1996(5)	0.158787	3.448765	26566	0.148661

DEF: default rate. Approximated by the percentage of bank claims on business in bad financial standing of total corporate outstanding debt to the 15 or 16 most important banks (in Introduction **Information Bulletins**). Note: NBP stopped publishing this figure in December 1995. For 1996 the rates are obtained by extrapolating rates for 1995.

EXCHR: exchange rate – the free-market average exchange rate (*EXCHR*: zloty/dollars, Table 1, **Information Bulletin**). These figures are used for calculating *PE*, the expected relative change in the exchange rate. *PE* is calculated as: $(EXCHR - EXCHR_{-1})/EXCHR_{-1}$.

P: price level. Approximated by consumer price index, Table 1, **Information Bulletin**. These figures are used for calculating the inflation rate $((P - P(-1))/P(-1))$.

htaxr: the direct tax rate for households. Calculated as *HTAX/LABINC* (see Tables A3 and A14).

Table A10 Required reserve ratios

Year (Month)	rat_3	rat_4	rat_1	rat_2
1991(12)	0	0	0.3	0.1
1992(1)	0	0	0.3	0.1
1992(2)	0	0	0.3	0.1
1992(3)	0	0	0.3	0.1
1992(4)	0	0	0.25	0.1
1992(5)	0	0	0.25	0.1
1992(6)	0	0	0.25	0.1
1992(7)	0	0	0.23	0.1
1992(8)	0	0	0.23	0.1
1992(9)	0	0	0.23	0.1
1992(10)	0	0	0.23	0.1
1992(11)	0	0	0.23	0.1
1992(12)	0	0	0.23	0.1
1993(1)	0	0	0.23	0.1
1993(2)	0	0	0.23	0.1
1993(3)	0	0	0.23	0.1
1993(4)	0	0	0.23	0.1
1993(5)	0	0	0.23	0.1
1993(6)	0	0	0.23	0.1
1993(7)	0	0	0.23	0.1
1993(8)	0	0	0.23	0.1
1993(9)	0	0	0.23	0.1
1993(10)	0	0	0.23	0.1
1993(11)	0	0	0.23	0.1
1993(12)	0	0	0.23	0.1
1994(1)	0	0	0.23	0.1
1994(2)	0.0075	0.005	0.23	0.1
1994(3)	0.0075	0.005	0.23	0.1
1994(4)	0.0075	0.005	0.23	0.1
1994(5)	0.0075	0.005	0.23	0.1
1994(6)	0.0075	0.005	0.23	0.1
1994(7)	0.0075	0.005	0.23	0.1
1994(8)	0.0075	0.005	0.23	0.1
1994(9)	0.0075	0.005	0.23	0.1
1994(10)	0.01	0.01	0.2	0.1
1994(11)	0.01	0.01	0.2	0.1
1994(12)	0.01	0.01	0.2	0.1
1995(1)	0.01	0.01	0.2	0.1
1995(2)	0.01	0.01	0.2	0.1
1995(3)	0.01	0.01	0.2	0.09
1995(4)	0.01	0.01	0.2	0.09
1995(5)	0.01	0.01	0.2	0.09
1995(6)	0.01	0.01	0.2	0.09
1995(7)	0.01	0.01	0.2	0.09
1995(8)	0.01	0.01	0.2	0.09
1995(9)	0.01	0.01	0.2	0.09
1995(10)	0.01	0.01	0.2	0.09
1995(11)	0.01	0.01	0.2	0.09
1995(12)	0.01	0.01	0.2	0.09

Table A10 – cont.

Year (Month)	rat_3	rat_4	rat_1	rat_2
1996(1)	0.01	0.01	0.2	0.09
1996(2)	0.02	0.02	0.2	0.09
1996(3)	0.02	0.02	0.2	0.09
1996(4)	0.02	0.02	0.2	0.09
1996(5)	0.02	0.02	0.2	0.09

rat_1: required reserve ratio on zloty demand deposits.
rat_2: required reserve ratio on zloty time deposits.
rat_3: required reserve ratio on foreign currency-denominated demand deposits.
rat_4: required reserve ratio on foreign currency-denominated time deposits.
All reserve ratios are obtained from the **Information Bulletins** (see Table 1).

Table A11 Nominal assets of firms

Year (Month)	CD	CTD	CFD	CFTD
1991(12)	46946.3	24306.9	2076.9	1090
1992(1)	47129.1	26260	2263.5	901.3
1992(2)	43002.2	27620.2	2386.4	1173.5
1992(3)	44892.8	30672.1	2425.1	1243.6
1992(4)	45297.5	32536.6	2105.9	1208.9
1992(5)	45555.6	33665.2	2145.6	1341.2
1992(6)	47623.7	37280.4	2160.2	1350.2
1992(7)	49753	40066.6	1322.7	2279.4
1992(8)	50852.4	41133.8	1108.1	2518.2
1992(9)	51093.4	43029.5	1228.2	2358.3
1992(10)	52578.2	45091.9	1406	2081.9
1992(11)	54119.4	45822.3	1523	2218
1992(12)	63792.6	45020.4	1303.6	2245.7
1993(1)	57292	47278.9	1391	2234.9
1993(2)	51913	48199	1281	2522.3
1993(3)	53603.6	48004.1	1301.4	2997.8
1993(4)	52677	49359.5	1130.7	3062.5
1993(5)	56967.9	48723.2	1203.2	3299.3
1993(6)	57711.7	48513.9	1426	3444.8
1993(7)	61206.3	49259.3	1598.1	3578.8
1993(8)	63981.7	50001.1	1363.3	4840.7
1993(9)	62464.2	50667.8	1316.4	4207.3
1993(10)	63900.7	52648	1287.9	4079.5
1993(11)	68917.2	52601.9	1324.5	4129.8
1993(12)	82488.2	53270.1	1489	5044.7
1994(1)	76253.7	54260.3	1553.2	5489
1994(2)	77599.3	58628.3	1985.6	5866.2
1994(3)	74189.7	60393.6	1345	6312.8
1994(4)	70508.8	63030.8	1513.7	5841.4
1994(5)	75638.4	62822.1	1426.8	6326.8
1994(6)	74914.9	67747.1	2325.5	6248.5
1994(7)	78133.3	71620.7	2424	7021
1994(8)	83834.9	77228.1	2210.7	7041.3
1994(9)	82175.5	81690.5	2567.9	6917.1
1994(10)	81090	82649	2556.8	6740.2
1994(11)	88839	82599	2749	6572
1994(12)	128874	79818	4882	6565
1995(1)	92687	84167	4700	6817
1995(2)	88704	85863	4136	7310
1995(3)	91827	87934	4419	7087
1995(4)	88164	91494	4612	7001
1995(5)	98129	92724	3657	6309
1995(6)	97126	96255	3571	5821
1995(7)	105551	97173	3901	6002
1995(8)	111035	101429	3404	5998
1995(9)	106343	103809	3943	5966
1995(10)	113293	106317	4318	5948
1995(11)	115942	103415	4047	5640
1995(12)	133485	104001	9604.5	6271.5

Table A11 – cont.

Year (Month)	CD	CTD	CFD	CFTD
1996(1)	119521	103786	9817.5	7435.5
1996(2)	115138.5	105243.5	10187	8015
1996(3)	114614	110921	10312	8736
1996(4)	111339	114475	11213	9777
1996(5)	117624.5	113475.5	11889	10063

DC = nominal corporate demand for (zloty) demand deposits.
CTD = nominal corporate demand for (zloty) time deposits.
CFD = nominal corporate demand for foreign currency demand deposits.
CFTD = nominal corporate demand for foreign currency time deposits.
All these figures are from the **Information Bulletins** (Table 2).
RCD, RCTD, RCFD and *RCFTD* used in the simulation model and the estimates are calculated by deflating the nominal corporate figures by the consumer price index. Δ*RCD*, Δ*RCTD*, Δ*RCFD* and Δ*RCFTD* used in model and estimates are derived by the first difference of the real stocks.

Table A12 Nominal assets and liabilities of firms

Year (Month)	CAPST	CNOA	L_f	ΔFDI
1991(12)	2026496	0	186280.5	80.948
1992(1)	2184269	3361.101	189054.2	22.774
1992(2)	2230298	13359.57	192797.1	65.255
1992(3)	2284644	21036.78	200676.8	40.881
1992(4)	2375965	31072.24	202415.5	117.8493
1992(5)	2481959	33718.18	202098.8	119.6433
1992(6)	2535310	46023.33	211559	117.1993
1992(7)	2576028	52893.77	214818.8	669.7053
1992(8)	2655911	62869.79	219139.1	676.46
1992(9)	2805560	65966.01	220550.5	686.5423
1992(10)	2904751	75835.47	224808.7	1247
1992(11)	2984912	69205.68	224109.5	1297
1992(12)	3074196	77617.65	236770	1323.25
1993(1)	3205360	98203.94	239043.1	141.534
1993(2)	3319700	113239.2	243570.1	145.917
1993(3)	3399066	131641.2	252396.4	150.363
1993(4)	3485651	149302.5	257667.2	367.8523
1993(5)	3562658	164294.3	260653.9	375.0213
1993(6)	3624533	194101.3	269421.7	395.5903
1993(7)	3675310	215379.1	274496	1522.164
1993(8)	3772310	239511.4	281788	1632.876
1993(9)	3879990	265358.8	288714.3	1637.58
1993(10)	3968096	297728	296092.5	1575.366
1993(11)	4144609	321079.9	301695.2	1603.524
1993(12)	4397277	329747.1	309304.8	1662.024
1994(1)	4483758	349638.8	316747.6	1538.064
1994(2)	4541610	356403.3	322138.1	259.188
1994(3)	4646325	373550.5	328817.7	630.286
1994(4)	4789364	394711.3	333251.3	1214.84
1994(5)	4886819	412951	335729.6	711.616
1994(6)	5014866	437705.9	343814	2023.203
1994(7)	5103364	467760.7	348505	1505.624
1994(8)	5203791	494675.4	350457	227.89
1994(9)	5458204	534970	356990	505.384
1994(10)	5637907	578540.9	365737	1123.619
1994(11)	5763236	601201.9	377451	343.182
1994(12)	5906086	583207.4	382144	2159.229
1995(1)	6158449	652613.4	391461	2157.93
1995(2)	6301702	675035.2	396905	1964.638
1995(3)	6419245	704998.2	411968	658.252
1995(4)	6582837	730926.7	419751	1725.088
1995(5)	6721228	745627.3	424872	762.729
1995(6)	6811563	771872.1	437871	674.54
1995(7)	6765675	781205.3	448916	4151.889
1995(8)	6814233	794738.4	459005	1160.592
1995(9)	7045864	829941.4	471947	391.472
1995(10)	7201084	850878.8	485626	1503.624
1995(11)	7325242	867563.4	502079	1595.75
1995(12)	7487470	853687.3	505892	10725.06

Table A12 – cont.

Year (Month)	CAPST	CNOA	L_f	ΔFDI
1996(1)	7726158	895045.8	512004	2171.607
1996(2)	7894224	937093.3	523762	10732.71
1996(3)	8037599	970929	531540	6456.24
1996(4)	8233038	1002606	539879	2605.7
1996(5)	8367132	1023247	544451	2948.826

CAPST = nominal capital stock. It is derived by multiplying the real capital stock (*RCAPST*) with the consumer price index. *RCAPST*, used in the model, is calculated by summing real investments ($\Delta RCAPST$: see below) and the lagged real capital stock. The starting value of the real capital stock is assumed to be equal to approximately 3 times real GDP.

CNOA = nominal value of net other assets held by firms. It is found by multiplying the real stock of net other assets for firms (*RCNOA*) with the consumer price index. *RCNOA* is calculated by summing the change in the real flow of net other assets ($\Delta RCNOA$: see Table A13 below) and the lagged stock of real net other assets. The starting value of the stock of real net other assets is assumed to be zero.

L_f = the nominal stock of bank loans to firms. The real stock (RL_f) is calculated by deflating the nominal stock by the consumer price index.

ΔFDI is the nominal **flow** of foreign direct investments, denominated in zloty. It is calculated by multiplying foreign direct investments, denominated in US dollars (given in **PlanEcon**) times the exchange rate. In the model we use the flow of direct investments in **real** terms ($\Delta RFDI$). $\Delta RFDI$ is derived by deflating ΔFDI by the consumer price index.

Table A13 Additional variables for firms

Year (Month)	ΔRCNOA	ΔRCAPST	RETAIN	IK
1991(12)	—	—	—	−0.01338
1992(1)	3126.605	5382.233	15696.61	−0.01612
1992(2)	9085.068	6785.467	12039.29	−0.01649
1992(3)	6638.488	8508.781	14713.6	−0.01055
1992(4)	8005.703	6384.169	18296.85	−0.01046
1992(5)	1149.265	7871.135	14570.14	−0.00932
1992(6)	9595.628	9904.143	17957.89	−0.00868
1992(7)	5055.51	6110.057	13332.85	−0.00794
1992(8)	6692.077	7260.944	14363.28	−0.00786
1992(9)	−156.686	7437.798	12124.7	−0.00819
1992(10)	5721.789	11227.22	18113.06	−0.00565
1992(11)	−5900.93	10592.83	8022.321	−0.00561
1992(12)	4776.565	16459.56	19392.59	−0.01582
1993(1)	11585.93	3409.627	14010.7	0.000666
1993(2)	7556.993	4232.251	8855.477	−0.00096
1993(3)	10077.48	5300.544	12855.81	−0.0022
1993(4)	9042.775	5710.962	13530.8	−0.00263
1993(5)	7385.348	7192.77	16655.02	−0.00138
1993(6)	16521.31	9081.93	21845.81	0.000834
1993(7)	11285.66	6001.129	17123.71	0.000319
1993(8)	11073.37	7162.182	17817.38	0.000279
1993(9)	11189.25	7534.113	15311.91	0.002087
1993(10)	15158.19	8601.696	22369.9	0.004029
1993(11)	5970.013	7973.308	16568.89	0.003475
1993(12)	−4563.5	11998.73	15339.37	−0.00467
1994(1)	6904.596	3626.068	5231.901	0.012215
1994(2)	1461.708	4602.507	7439.427	0.011589
1994(3)	4735.898	5769.724	7860.662	0.01437
1994(4)	4890.815	4796.856	8911.663	0.015501
1994(5)	5176.428	6047.958	13751.05	0.015626
1994(6)	6882.901	7564.403	14100.22	0.018902
1994(7)	10344.01	5583.912	17993.24	0.017328
1994(8)	8303.685	6705.973	20258.07	0.020346
1994(9)	7346.129	6914.641	16016.32	0.02209
1994(10)	11353.86	8963.143	18344.89	0.022555
1994(11)	4754.553	8490.051	12934.42	0.022731
1994(12)	−11413.2	13231.95	15913.43	0.017133
1995(1)	16996.29	3815.68	7138.316	0.020599
1995(2)	3157.276	4794.192	5948.532	0.024054
1995(3)	6902.191	6036.142	10383.59	0.027718
1995(4)	3381.931	5279.015	7114.023	0.025559
1995(5)	508.5926	6652.559	9857.453	0.025
1995(6)	6488.921	8427.474	11654.23	0.025
1995(7)	5810.196	6937.549	10113.77	0.026
1995(8)	3704.949	8440.345	11742.11	0.026
1995(9)	3768.47	8834.563	9928.841	0.027
1995(10)	2191.078	11195.03	13045.54	0.026
1995(11)	1913.93	10664.35	7501.733	0.026
1995(12)	−8606.86	16683.81	12516.86	0.02

Table A13 – cont.

Year (Month)	$\Delta RCNOA$	$\Delta RCAPST$	RETAIN	IK
1996(1)	4889.86	4367.013	5061.983	0.015
1996(2)	7513.729	5496.149	7162.888	0.015
1996(3)	5867.31	6925.085	11625.4	0.021
1996(4)	3150.61	6466.92	8873.821	0.021
1996(5)	2247.855	8191.735	11163.01	0.021

$\Delta RCNOA$: the real change in net other assets for firms is calculated from the budget constraint of firms as $RETAIN - \Delta RCD - \Delta RCTD - \Delta RCFD - \Delta RCFTD - \Delta RCAPST + \Delta RL_f + \Delta RFDI$.

$\Delta RCAPST$ = real investments. Real investments are found by deflating the monthly series on total gross adjusted nominal investments ($TINVA$: see Table A15 below) by the consumer price index.

$RETAIN$: real retained earnings of firms: calculated as real GDP ($RGDP$: see below) minus nominal labour income ($LABINC$: see Table A14 below) deflated by the consumer price index minus real corporate taxes (calculated as nominal corporate taxes, CIT, deflated by the consumer price index).

IK = profit rate. Approximated by the pre-tax profitability index. See **Information Bulletin** (Table 1).

Table A14 Determination of tax rate for firms

Year (Month)	CIT	ctaxr	GDP	LABINC
1991(12)	—	—	—	—
1992(1)	1442	0.07873	58269.4	39953.54
1992(2)	4539	0.256296	57319.42	39609.43
1992(3)	4615	0.219392	64778.45	43743.08
1992(4)	3740	0.150144	70132.5	45223.04
1992(5)	4095	0.189255	64659.89	43022.44
1992(6)	2736	0.110695	69094.07	44377.61
1992(7)	5201	0.239305	68816.88	47083.15
1992(8)	4146	0.18472	69738.64	47293.82
1992(9)	3611	0.181729	69498.2	49627.97
1992(10)	4335	0.147704	81896.94	52547.8
1992(11)	5083	0.30974	72902.69	56492.17
1992(12)	7123	0.202897	96809.42	61702.92
1993(1)	628	0.028974	74598.59	52924.23
1993(2)	4931	0.263963	74486.76	55806.15
1993(3)	6504	0.241861	89109.61	62218.14
1993(4)	5656	0.204912	89456.2	61854.16
1993(5)	4125	0.130361	91977.61	60334.6
1993(6)	4159	0.102121	101934.4	61208.1
1993(7)	6147	0.174972	97055.3	61924.04
1993(8)	4908	0.137246	99051.26	63290.68
1993(9)	5086	0.157642	97322.47	65059.51
1993(10)	6475	0.137996	114155.6	67234.04
1993(11)	5332	0.146045	108404.4	71895.15
1993(12)	8621	0.220608	121819.4	82741.03
1994(1)	1193	0.101374	83878.37	72110.09
1994(2)	4935	0.245097	93231.35	73096.49
1994(3)	6852	0.294833	107196.3	83956
1994(4)	7543	0.283004	109194.2	82540.88
1994(5)	4478	0.129855	112806	78321.24
1994(6)	4054	0.114125	117158.2	81635.64
1994(7)	5574	0.120289	128346.8	82008.53
1994(8)	4526	0.088423	133054.4	81868.88
1994(9)	5790	0.130508	130175.6	85810.39
1994(10)	6320	0.122059	140849.4	89070.99
1994(11)	6530	0.166701	136699.7	97527.64
1994(12)	10460	0.203588	162022.1	110643.7
1995(1)	820	0.041149	114889.3	94961.96
1995(2)	8110	0.332798	121534.1	97164.96
1995(3)	8760	0.233007	144585.3	106989.9
1995(4)	7610	0.273514	138354.7	110531.6
1995(5)	6220	0.179071	144848.1	110113.2
1995(6)	5750	0.144501	150688.3	110896.2
1995(7)	7980	0.214307	148122.8	110886.5
1995(8)	8050	0.191041	155103.9	112966.5
1995(9)	7850	0.209102	153402.7	115861.2
1995(10)	7060	0.15104	167921.5	121178.8
1995(11)	8330	0.264961	161509.3	130070.8
1995(12)	11580	0.228328	189740.2	139023.5

Table A14 – cont.

Year (Month)	CIT	ctaxr	GDP	LABINC
1996(1)	1200	0.068563	141289.1	123786.9
1996(2)	10420	0.307048	159277.3	125341.2
1996(3)	10350	0.210801	181518.9	132420.6
1996(4)	8860	0.226742	176928.9	137853.6
1996(5)	6410	0.142734	184420.4	139511.8

CIT: nominal corporate income taxes. Taken from **PlanEcon**.
ctaxr: corporate tax rate. Calculated by $CIT/(GDP - LABINC)$.
GDP = nominal Gross Domestic Product. Calculated by multiplying real GDP (*RGDP*: see Table A16 below) with the consumer price index.
LABINC = nominal labour income. Calculated by multiplying employment (*H*: see Table A3) with gross wages (*W*: see Table A3).

Table A15 Determination of monthly nominal investments

Year (Month)	TINV	PUBINV	PRIVINV	CORRECT	TINVA
1991(12)	55477	34481.15	20995.85	—	—
1992(1)	22705	14112.06	8592.945	0.254829	5785.9
1992(2)	22705	14112.06	8592.945	0.326946	7423.3
1992(3)	22705	14112.06	8592.945	0.418225	9495.799
1992(4)	28986	18015.94	10970.06	0.254829	7386.484
1992(5)	28986	18015.94	10970.06	0.326946	9476.846
1992(6)	28986	18015.94	10970.06	0.418225	12122.67
1992(7)	26801	19370	7431	0.282694	7576.47
1992(8)	26801	19370	7431	0.345153	9250.443
1992(9)	26801	19370	7431	0.372154	9974.087
1992(10)	54213	32474	21739	0.285998	15504.78
1992(11)	54213	32474	21739	0.275895	14957.08
1992(12)	54213	32474	21739	0.438108	23751.14
1993(1)	20099	13317	6782	0.254829	5121.815
1993(2)	20099	13317	6782	0.326946	6571.28
1993(3)	20099	13317	6782	0.418225	8405.905
1993(4)	36349	23664	12685	0.254829	9262.792
1993(5)	36349	23664	12685	0.326946	11884.15
1993(6)	36349	23664	12685	0.418225	15202.06
1993(7)	35932	23511	12421	0.282694	10157.74
1993(8)	35932	23511	12421	0.345153	12402.03
1993(9)	35932	23511	12421	0.372154	13372.22
1993(10)	54380	40170	14210	0.285998	15552.55
1993(11)	54380	40170	14210	0.275895	15003.15
1993(12)	54380	40170	14210	0.438108	23824.3
1994(1)	28762	19580	9182	0.254829	7329.402
1994(2)	28762	19580	9182	0.326946	9403.61
1994(3)	28762	19580	9182	0.418225	12028.99
1994(4)	40366	26931	13435	0.254829	10286.44
1994(5)	40366	26931	13435	0.326946	13197.49
1994(6)	40366	26931	13435	0.418225	16882.07
1994(7)	44750	30675	14075	0.282694	12650.54
1994(8)	44750	30675	14075	0.345153	15445.59
1994(9)	44750	30675	14075	0.372154	16653.87
1994(10)	77660	53971	23689	0.285998	22210.57
1994(11)	77660	53971	23689	0.275895	21425.98
1994(12)	77660	53971	23689	0.438108	34023.45
1995(1)	40080	24356	15724	0.254829	10213.56
1995(2)	40080	24356	15724	0.326946	13103.98
1995(3)	40080	24356	15724	0.418225	16762.46
1995(4)	58860	37020	21840	0.254829	14999.26
1995(5)	58860	37020	21840	0.326946	19244.02
1995(6)	58860	37020	21840	0.418225	24616.72
1995(7)	70990	46767	24223	0.282694	20068.42
1995(8)	70990	46767	24223	0.345153	24502.4
1995(9)	70990	46767	24223	0.372154	26419.18
1995(10)	119070	79457	39613	0.285998	34053.73
1995(11)	119070	79457	39613	0.275895	32850.77
1995(12)	119070	79457	39613	0.438108	52165.5

Table A15 – cont.

Year (Month)	TINV	PUBINV	PRIVINV	CORRECT	TINVA
1996(1)	55190	31603	23587	0.254829	14064.03
1996(2)	55190	31603	23587	0.326946	18044.13
1996(3)	55190	31603	23587	0.418225	23081.84
1996(4)	86410	51958	34452	0.254829	22019.8
1996(5)	86410	51958	34452	0.326946	28251.37

TINV = total gross nominal investment on a quarterly basis.
PUBINV and *PRIVINV* are the division of total gross investment over public investments (*PUBINV*) and private investments (*PRIVINV*).
TINV, *PUBINV* and *PRIVINV* are taken from different issues of the **Statistical Bulletin**. *PUBINV* and *PRIVINV* are here only presented for reasons of completeness: in the model no distinction is made between *PUBINV* and *PRIVINV*.
Total gross investments on a quarterly basis are reconverted in a series on a monthly basis (*TINVA*) by using *CORRECT*.
CORRECT is derived from monthly data on investment expenditures for 1991 (this was the only year for which we could find monthly data on investment, given in **PlanEcon** Report, 4 June 1992).

Table A16 Determination of real GDP

Year (Month)	RGDP	C	RTB	sharegov	TB
1991(12)	—	37902.92	−6221.43	—	−538
1992(1)	54204.09	38194.71	328.3693	0.19	31
1992(2)	52394.35	33733.29	1920.668	0.19	161
1992(3)	58045.21	36151.2	2356.641	0.19	193
1992(4)	60615.82	39682.42	3032.225	0.19	258
1992(5)	53704.23	34230.44	1398.846	0.19	122
1992(6)	56449.41	33820.15	1999.725	0.19	181
1992(7)	55497.49	37994.72	848.1871	0.19	78
1992(8)	54739.9	37270.81	−192.433	0.19	−18
1992(9)	51825.65	34406.97	134.0037	0.19	13
1992(10)	59302.64	37143.82	−335.904	0.19	−31
1992(11)	51630.8	34027.87	−2799.76	0.19	−254
1992(12)	67089	40325.45	−2442.92	0.19	−222
1993(1)	49660.78	37148.7	−2816.14	0.24	−269
1993(2)	47973.4	33021.13	−793.594	0.24	−76
1993(3)	56190.19	37667.38	−263.375	0.24	−25
1993(4)	55154.1	37871.6	−1665.45	0.24	−164
1993(5)	55668.6	37778.12	−2662.76	0.24	−262
1993(6)	60897.06	40681.31	−3481.48	0.24	−329
1993(7)	57339.63	40992.13	−3415.14	0.24	−319
1993(8)	57202.16	38455.63	−2144.17	0.24	−191
1993(9)	54832.96	37214.39	−3075.46	0.24	−280
1993(10)	63136.39	39761.76	−379.794	0.24	−34
1993(11)	57610.66	36761.3	−950.509	0.24	−87
1993(12)	61352.42	37387.08	−2757.98	0.24	−257
1994(1)	41497.07	32100.24	−2113.68	0.19	−200
1994(2)	45631.2	31830.19	528.5712	0.19	50
1994(3)	51416.87	37108.06	−1230.12	0.19	−118
1994(4)	50920.3	36716.39	−267.807	0.19	−26
1994(5)	51695.12	36090.05	−264.964	0.19	−26
1994(6)	52495.45	36092.58	−1135.67	0.19	−114
1994(7)	56651.92	38994.83	1309.318	0.19	132
1994(8)	57767.91	40323.5	−237.462	0.19	−24
1994(9)	54048.55	38009.24	−1144.55	0.19	−120
1994(10)	56840.21	37586.39	−508.963	0.19	−55
1994(11)	54167.3	36113.96	−728.496	0.19	−75
1994(12)	63011.47	40260.51	−2453.17	0.19	−260
1995(1)	42921.46	32644.43	−2122.94	0.2	−237
1995(2)	44464.19	31750.14	−972.98	0.2	−111
1995(3)	52064.99	35590.45	25.39669	0.2	3
1995(4)	48694.18	32987.14	689.1948	0.2	84
1995(5)	50073.26	33853.49	−447.443	0.2	−56
1995(6)	51587.76	34084.96	−1242.23	0.2	−156
1995(7)	51205.29	34472.68	−445.993	0.2	−55
1995(8)	53428.66	35843.44	−1540.85	0.2	−185
1995(9)	51297.81	33979.13	−1775.44	0.2	−217
1995(10)	55203.57	34394.94	−1427.12	0.2	−179
1995(11)	52430.77	32985.78	−1705.51	0.2	−214
1995(12)	60683.58	35883.49	−4020.44	0.2	−504

Table A16 – cont.

Year (Month)	RGDP	C	RTB	sharegov	TB
1996(1)	43871.6	35853.43	−5123.16	0.2	−661
1996(2)	48515.04	36392.26	−3076.37	0.2	−399
1996(3)	54459.87	39579.09	−2936.28	0.2	−382
1996(4)	51961.62	39081.72	−3979.35	0.2	−520
1996(5)	53474.32	39587	−4999.28	0.2	−649

RGDP = real Gross Domestic Product. It is calculated as real consumption (*C*), plus real investment (Δ*RCAPST*: see above), plus the real trade balance (*RTB*) over one minus share of government consumption in GDP (*sharegov*).

C: real household consumption. It is approximated by deflating nominal consumption with the consumer price index. Nominal consumption is calculated by using quarterly figures on the average monthly per capita expenditures by employees' households (see below) and population figures (see Table A4). These quarterly data are intrapolated in monthly figures by using the corrected retail sales of goods index (see Table A17 below).

RTB is calculated by multiplying the Hard-Currency trade balance, BOP (balance of payments) basis, in current US dollars (*TB*), (given in **PlanEcon**) by the exchange rate, and deflating by the consumer price index. The exact formula is: $RTB = TB*ER/ (1000*P)$.

Sharegov is taken from different issues of **PlanEcon**. This figure is only available on a yearly basis. For 1995 and 1996 it is an estimate.

Table A17 Help variables determination of household consumption and nominal foreign reserves

Year (Month)	PCEXP	PCEXPADJ	RATP	FRES
1991(12)	989400	989400	—	37011.4
1992(1)	1029000	1071541	1.041342	35507.4
1992(2)	1029000	962978.3	0.935839	41251.6
1992(3)	1029000	1052481	1.022819	45282.8
1992(4)	1117000	1197417	1.071994	48395.1
1992(5)	1117000	1074582	0.962025	49281.5
1992(6)	1117000	1079001	0.965981	51806.5
1992(7)	1222000	1227584	1.00457	56561.2
1992(8)	1222000	1236891	1.012186	61409.3
1992(9)	1222000	1201525	0.983244	58476
1992(10)	1367000	1335545	0.97699	58570.8
1992(11)	1367000	1250810	0.915004	57221.1
1992(12)	1367000	1514645	1.108007	57576.3
1993(1)	1447000	1452419	1.003745	50949.6
1993(2)	1447000	1334275	0.922097	51504.8
1993(3)	1447000	1554306	1.074157	48203.3
1993(4)	1664000	1597991	0.960331	48141.3
1993(5)	1664000	1623406	0.975605	50202.2
1993(6)	1664000	1770603	1.064064	48687.1
1993(7)	1750000	1803563	1.030608	52043
1993(8)	1750000	1730413	0.988808	58162
1993(9)	1750000	1716023	0.980585	63874.9
1993(10)	1864000	1867432	1.001841	68949.2
1993(11)	1864000	1796647	0.963867	69398.2
1993(12)	1864000	1927921	1.034292	78037.3
1994(1)	1794000	1684961	0.93922	81651.3
1994(2)	1794000	1688664	0.941284	85632.5
1994(3)	1794000	2008375	1.119495	92136.1
1994(4)	2059000	2043582	0.992512	95908.9
1994(5)	2059000	2043582	0.992512	95994.7
1994(6)	2059000	2089836	1.014976	93677.4
1994(7)	2358000	2291556	0.971822	105722.7
1994(8)	2358000	2408721	1.02151	117382.3
1994(9)	2358000	2373723	1.006668	116780.3
1994(10)	2487000	2414921	0.971018	93046.3
1994(11)	2487000	2362834	0.950074	112457
1994(12)	2487000	2683245	1.078908	114186
1995(1)	2359000	2265327	0.960291	122062
1995(2)	2359000	2249715	0.953673	142679
1995(3)	2359000	2561958	1.086036	157090
1995(4)	2516000	2429527	0.965631	192517
1995(5)	2516000	2538265	1.00885	208882
1995(6)	2516000	2580207	1.02552	226639
1995(7)	2637000	2583753	0.979808	258886
1995(8)	2637000	2695416	1.022153	288682
1995(9)	2637000	2631830	0.99804	314281
1995(10)	2749000	2709570	0.985657	328528
1995(11)	2749000	2631439	0.957235	354786

Table A17 – cont.

Year (Month)	PCEXP	PCEXPADJ	RATP	FRES
1995(12)	2749000	2905991	1.057108	366925
1996(1)	3168000	2991283	0.944218	393128
1996(2)	3168000	3095274	0.977044	433073
1996(3)	3168000	3417443	1.078738	451391
1996(4)	3491400	3446949	0.987269	460201
1996(5)	3491400	3535851	1.012731	481183

PCEXP: unadjusted quarterly figures on the average monthly per capita expenditures by employees' households (**PlanEcon**).

PCEXPADJ: adjusted quarterly figures on the average monthly per capita expenditures by employees' households. These figures are found by multiplying *PCEXP* with *RATP*, which is a help variable used to convert quarterly figures on per capita expenditures into monthly figures on per capita expenditures. It is derived by using figures on the corrected retail sales of goods index (**PlanEcon**).

FRES: Net nominal foreign reserves (net foreign assets) held by the central bank. It is calculated as Due From Abroad minus Foreign Liabilities (Table 3, **Information Bulletin**).

NOTES AND APPENDICES

3 Commercial banks

1 An earlier version of this chapter is published as Gupta and Lensink (1997) in Gupta (1997).

4 Households

Appendix

See Table A4.1 on pp. 166–7.

Note

1 Some authors have used an optimization framework which leads to a Purvis-like portfolio model. An example of such a model is Parkin *et al.* (1975), in which households' integrated consumption-savings and portfolio-allocation decision is derived from a model in which households are assumed to optimize intertemporal utility from consumption and asset holdings. Sterken (1991) also derives the integrated portfolio-allocation and consumption-savings model from an optimizing framework. His approach is somewhat simpler, but on many points similar to the one used by Parkin *et al.* (1975). The approach is comparable to the choice-theoretic approach used to derive the portfolio models for commercial banks, as explained in the previous chapter. It starts by assuming that households optimize a utility function of the following form:

$$E(U) = a - ce^{-b(c + m'v)}; \quad b,c > 0; \quad u' > 0; \quad u'' < 0$$

where a, b and c are parameters, c is real consumption, v is a $k \times 1$ vector of assets and liabilities (liabilities are measured as negative assets); m' is a $1 \times k$ vector of returns on assets, with mean m and variance $E(e_i e_j)$; ' denotes a row vector and U is a utility index. This utility function is then to be optimized subject to the flow budget constraint of households. If it is assumed that households face quadratic adjustment costs, that reducing consumption in order to buy assets, in contrast to reducing assets in order to increase consumption, has no costs and that the stochastic returns are normally distributed, the decision problem can be rewritten in a form similar to the one explained in Chapter 3. The decision problem can then be

Table A4.1: Preferred model results: "sequential estimates"

	ΔRHFTD	ΔRHFD	ΔRHTD	ΔRHD	ΔRCUR	ΔRHNFA	C
$(1 - htaxr_{-1})ID_{-1}$				178845 (2.67)			−3865385 (−4.95)
$(1 - htaxr)ITD$		−157110 (−2.64)	608689 (5.32)				
$(1 - htaxr)IFD$		1104671 (2.28)					
$(1 - htaxr)IFTD$	289661 (1.63)	−771244 (−3.58)					
$(1 - htaxr)IFO$	−384273 (−3.09)			−426854 (−4.24)			
pe	29043 (5.49)	17116 (6.57)					
π			−65069 (−6.06)		−76209 (−5.44)		
Y		0.131 (3.14)	0.122 (1.69)	0.092 (−5.29)	0.244 (3.42)		
$RHNW$							0.572 (5.04)

$RHFTD_{-1}$							
$RHFD_{-1}$		−0.049 (−2.33)	−0.143 (−6.32)	−0.014 (−2.31)			
$RHTD_{-1}$		−0.034 (−4.31)	−0.052 (−2.52)		−0.150 (−2.07)	0.540 (2.30)	
RHD_{-1}							
$RCUR_{-1}$			−0.024 (−7.70)	−0.058 (−5.02)	−0.291 (−4.16)		
$RHNFA_{-1}$					0.035 (2.31)	−0.925 (−4.88)	0.256 (3.30)
$RHNOA_{-1}$				0.002 (6.63)	0.018 (2.30)	−0.456 (−4.73)	0.019 (5.31)
Constant						253718 (4.52)	
Obs.	53	53	53	52	53	53	53
R^2	0.48	0.45	0.70	0.57	0.60	0.29	0.38
DW	2.25	1.60	1.06	2.12	2.06	1.88	1.14

written as maximizing the following expression, subject to the real budget constraint (see also Sterken, 1991)

$$MAX\ L = \mathbf{m}\cdot v - \frac{1}{2}[nc^2 + n'(v - v_0)c + (v - v_0)C(v - v_0)] - \frac{1}{2}bv\cdot Sv$$

where C is a (symmetrical) cost matrix, determining costs of selling one asset in order to be able to buy another asset, S is the variance–covariance matrix of returns on the assets, n is a scalar determining adjustment costs with respect to consumption and n' is a vector of adjustment costs from selling assets to increase consumption. This decision problem results in a set of desired asset holdings and an equation for real consumption, which depend on the real asset returns, the lagged real asset holdings and real income.

Although this approach is appealing, we do not follow it due to its shortcomings, which have already been brought forward in the previous chapter.

6 The complete model

Appendix 6.1: list of variables

If not indicated otherwise, variables are in "real" terms. With respect to financial variables, the variables given below refer to "stocks." The corresponding flow starts with a Δ.

Endogenous variables

C	= household consumption
$EXCH$	= nominal exchange rate (an increase is a depreciation)
H	= employment
P	= nominal goods price
pe	= expected and actual rate of depreciation
PW	= relative change in gross wages
Y	= disposable income of households
$RCAPST$	= capital stock
$RCBNFA$	= net foreign assets held by commercial banks
$RCBL$	= commercial bank borrowing from central bank
$RCBNW$	= net wealth of commercial banks
RCD	= zloty demand deposits held by firms
$RCEBGOV$	= central bank lending to government
$RCFD$	= foreign currency-denominated demand deposits held by firms
$RCFTD$	= foreign currency-denominated time deposits held by firms
$RCNOA$	= net other assets held by firms
$RCTAX$	= direct taxes paid by firms
$RCTD$	= zloty time deposits held by firms
$RCUR$	= currency held by households
$RCUR_s$	= currency supply
$REXCHR$	= real exchange rate
RER	= excess reserves of commercial banks
$RETAIN$	= retained earnings for firms
$REXNOA$	= net other assets held by external sector
$RFCDNS$	= foreign currency-denominated deposits of non-financial sectors

RFRES	= foreign reserves held by central bank
RGDP	= gross domestic product
RGOV	= commercial bank loans to the government
RHD	= zloty demand deposits held by households
RHFD	= foreign currency-denominated demand deposits held by households
RHFTD	= foreign currency-denominated time deposits held by households
RHNFA	= net foreign assets held by households
RHNOA	= net other assets held by households
RHTAX	= direct taxes paid by households
RHTD	= zloty time deposits held by households
RLABINC	= labour income
RL_f	= bank loans to firms
RREQRES	= required reserves of commercial banks
RPROD	= real production
RSTOCK	= real stock of goods
RTDEM	= real total demand for goods, which equals real sales of goods
RTRADEB	= trade balance
RZDNS	= zloty deposit of non-financial sectors
UNR	= rate of unemployment
W	= gross nominal wage rate
π	= inflation

The number of endogenous variables listed above is smaller than the number of equations. That is because we have not listed the flow variables corresponding to the listed stock variables.

Exogenous variables

ctaxr	= direct tax rate for firms
DEF	= default rate
htaxr	= household direct tax rate
ICB	= nominal rate of return on commercial bank borrowing from the central bank (the central bank: "discount rate")
ID	= nominal rate of return on zloty demand deposits
IE	= nominal rate of return on foreign assets held by commercial banks and households
IF	= nominal rate of return on bank loans to firms
IFD	= nominal rate of return on foreign currency-denominated demand deposits
IFTD	= nominal rate of return on foreign currency-denominated time deposits
IG	= nominal rate of return on commercial bank loans to government
IK	= nominal profit rate
ITD	= nominal rate of return on zloty time deposits
LABF	= labour force
$rat_1; rat_2; rat_3; rat_4$	= required reserve ratios on zloty demand deposits, zloty time deposits, foreign currency-denominated demand deposits and foreign currency-denominated time deposits
RCBNOA	= net other assets held by commercial banks
RCEBNOL	= net other liabilities of the central bank
RFDEBT	= foreign debt of government
RFDI	= foreign direct investments
RGOVCON	= government consumption

RGNOL	= net other liabilities of government
RTR	= transfers to households
share	= share of government consumption in *RGDP*

Some variables used in figures/descriptions, which are not used in full model

RATFA	= the ratio of central bank gross foreign assets to total assets
RATCBRER	= *RER/RTCBFINA*
RATCBGOV	= *RGOV/RTCBFINA*
RATCBLF	= RL_f/*RTCBFINA*
RATLCOMB	= the ratio of NBP lending to commercial banks
RATLGOV	= the ratio of direct lending by the NBP to the central government
RATOA	= the ratio of other assets of the NBP
RATRCUR	= *RCUR/RHTFINA*
RATRHD	= *RHD/RHTFINA*
RATRHFD	= *RHFD/RHTFINA*
RATRHFTD	= *RHFTD/RHTFINA*
RATRHTD	= *RHTD/RHTFINA*
RATTBILL	= the ratio of T-bills held by the NBP
RATTBONDS	= the ratio of bonds held by the NBP
RATTGOV	= total gross lending by the NBP to the central government
RTCBFINA	= $RNFA + RL_f + RGOVB + RER$ = total financial assets of commercial banks
RTCFINA	= $RCTD + RCD + RCFTD + RCFD$ = total demand for financial assets of firms
RTHFINA	= $RHTD + RHD + RCUR + RHFTD + RHFD$ = total demand for financial assets by households

Appendix 6.2: some ex-post *within-sample simulations*

See Figures A6.2.1 to A6.2.16 on following pages.

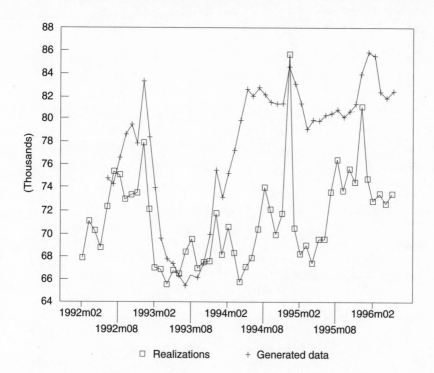

Figure A6.2.1 RTCFINA

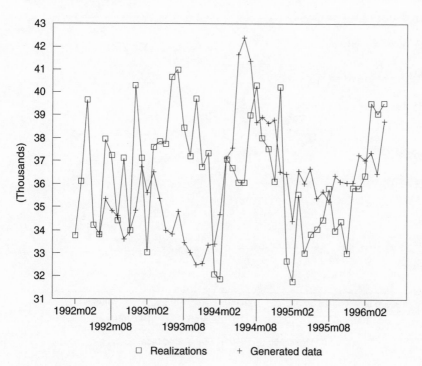

Figure A6.2.2 C

171

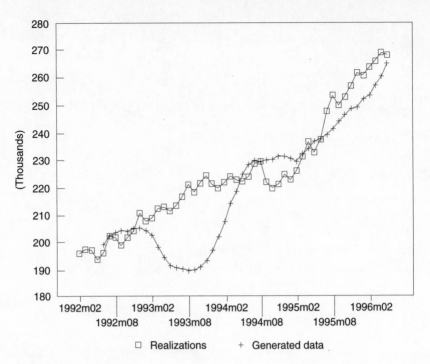

Figure A6.2.3 RTHFINA

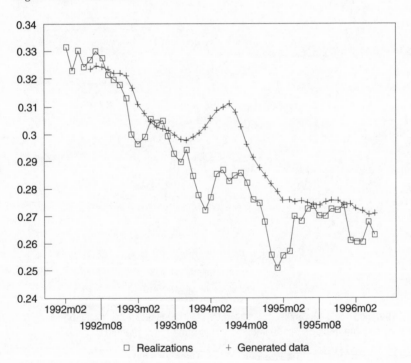

Figure A6.2.4 RATRCUR

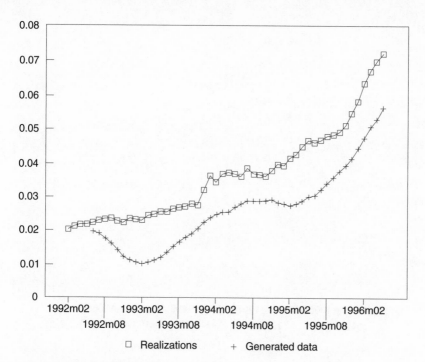

Figure A6.2.5 RATRHD

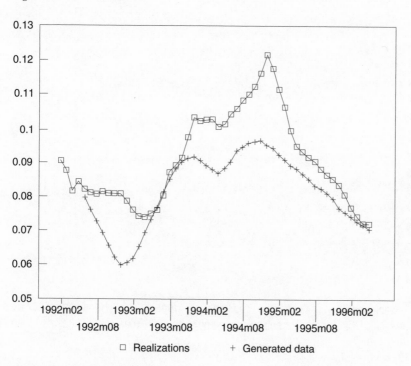

Figure A6.2.6 RATRHFD

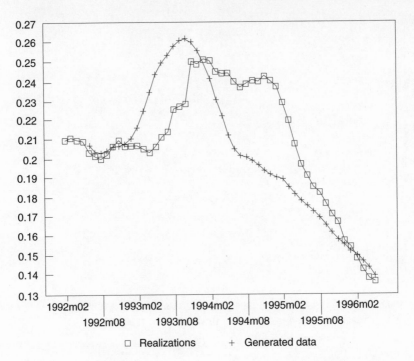

Figure A6.2.7 RATRHFTD

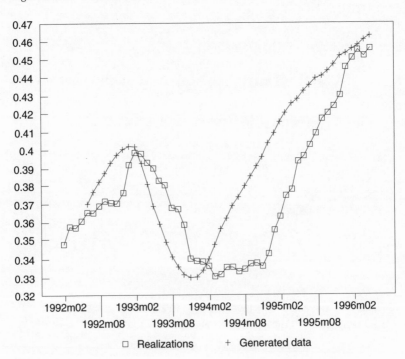

Figure A6.2.8 RATRHTD

174

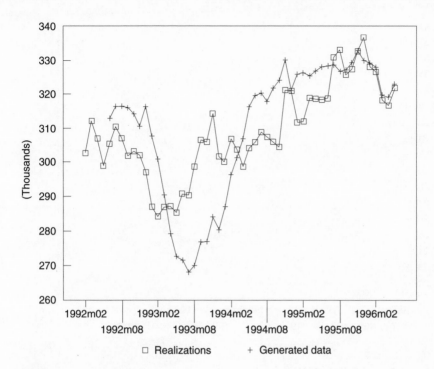

Figure A6.2.9 RTCBFINA

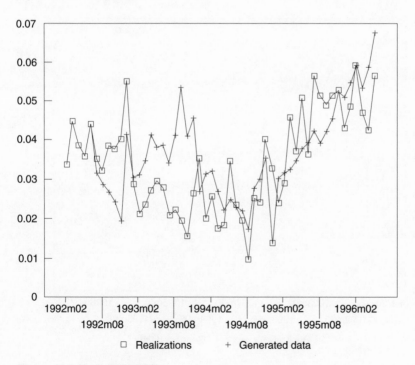

Figure A6.2.10 RATCBRER

175

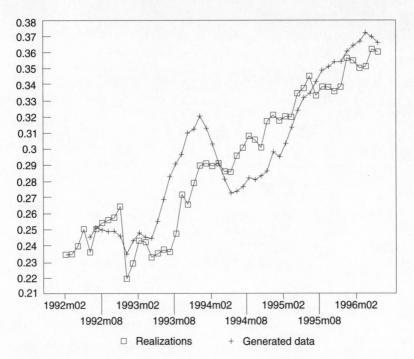

Figure A6.2.11 RATCBGOV

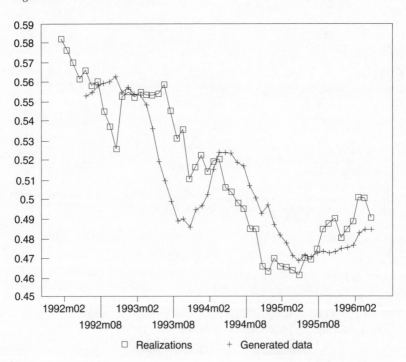

Figure A6.2.12 RATCBLF

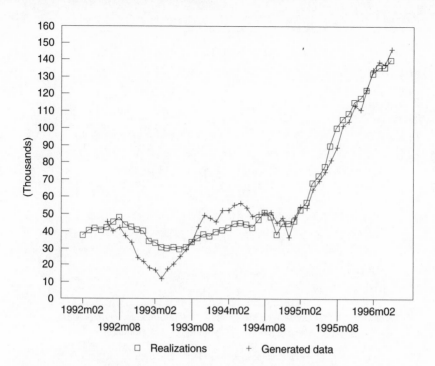

Figure A6.2.13 RFRES

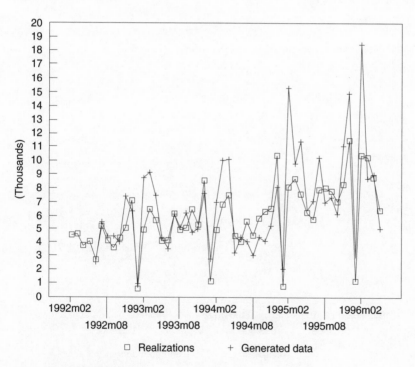

Figure A6.2.14 RCTAX

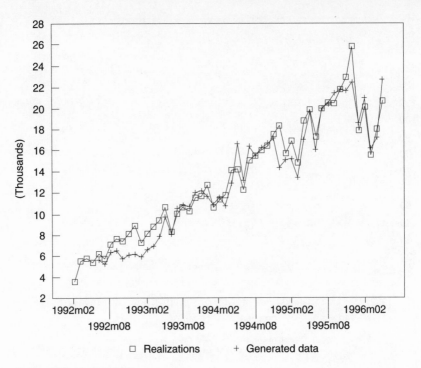

Figure A6.2.15 RHTAX

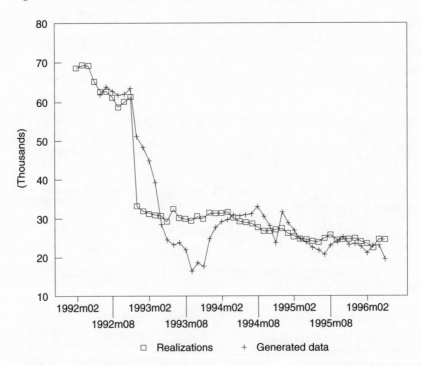

Figure A6.2.16 RCBL

Notes

1 A very early and preliminary version of this chapter was presented at the Poznan Conference in January 1996, and it was published as Gupta and Lensink (1996b) in proceedings edited by Janc and Kowalski, 1996.
2 In an earlier version of the model we estimated the demand for labour function by using the marginal productivity condition. However, the simulation results based on those estimates proved to be too unreasonable, which led us to use equation **(6.60).**
3 It should be noted that interest payments have not been included in any of the budget constraints and, therefore, in any of the behavioural equations. This is for two reasons. First, the data for interest payments were not available in all sectors. Second, as our model is specified in real terms, the estimates of interest payments in real terms, even if they had been available, were too erratic, because the real interest rates are essentially inflation-driven.

7 Some policy simulations

1 In all simulations the exogenous variables are assumed to take the values of May 1996, except for *ctaxr*, *htaxr*, $\Delta RGNOL$ and $\Delta RFDI$, which are assumed to be equal to the average value of the period January 1992–May 1996 (see the Appendix).

BIBLIOGRAPHY

Adam, Jan, "The Transition to a Market Economy in Poland," *Cambridge Journal of Economics* 18 (1994), 607–618.

Aslund, Anders, "Lessons of the First Four Years of Systematic Change in Eastern Europe," *Journal of Comparative Economics* 19, 1 (August 1994), 22–38.

Atkinson, Anthony B. and John Micklewright, *Economic Transformation in Eastern Europe and the Distribution of Income* (Cambridge: Cambridge University Press, 1992).

Baldassari, Mario, Luigi Pagnetto and Edmond S. Phelps, eds, *Privatization Processes in Eastern Europe* (New York: St Martin's Press, 1993).

Balino, Tomas J.J., Juhi Dhawan and V. Sundarajan, "The Payments Systems Reforms and Monetary Policy in Emerging Market Economies in Central and Eastern Europe," *IMF Working Paper* 94/13 (Washington: International Monetary Fund, January 1994).

Baltensberger, E., "Alternative Approaches to the Theory of the Banking Firm," *Journal of Monetary Economics* 6 (1980), 1–37.

Bank Gdanski S.A., *The Financial System in Poland* (Gdansk, 1995).

Berg, Andrew and Oliver Jean Blanchard, "Stabilization and Transition: Poland, 1990–91," in Oliver Jean Blanchard, Kenneth A. Froot and Jeffrey D. Sachs, eds, *The Transition in Eastern Europe* vol. 1 (Chicago: University of Chicago Press, 1994), 51–91.

Blanchard, Oliver J., "Transition in Poland," *The Economic Journal* 104 (Sept. 1994a), 1169–1177.

—— *Macroeconomics* (Upper Saddle River, N.J.: Prentice Hall, 1997).

——, Kenneth A. Froot and Jeffrey D. Sachs, eds, *The Transition in Eastern Europe: Country Studies* vol. 1 (Chicago: University of Chicago Press, 1994b).

—— *The Transition in Eastern Europe: Restructuring* vol. 2 (Chicago: University of Chicago Press, 1994c).

Blejer, Mario I., Guillermo A. Calvo, Fabrizio Coricelli and Alan H. Gelb, eds, *Proceedings of a Conference on the Macroeconomic Aspects of Adjustment*, co-sponsored by the IMF and the World Bank (Washington, IMF, 1993).

Blommestein, Hans J. and Michael G. Spencer, "The Role of Financial Institutions in the Transition to a Market Economy," in *Building Sound Finance in Emerging Market Economies*, Gerard Caprio *et al.*, eds (Washington: International Monetary Fund and World Bank, 1994).

—— "The Role of Financial Institutions in the Transition to a Market Economy," *IMF Working Paper* 93/75 (1993).

Bonin, John P., "On the Way to Privatizing Commercial Banks: Poland and Hungary Take Different Roads," *Comparative Economic Studies* 35 (Winter 1993), 103–120.

Bossak, Jan W., ed., *Poland: International Economic Report, 1992/93* (Warsaw: Wald Economy Research Institute, Warsaw School of Economics, 1993).

Borensztein, Eduardo and Peter Montiel, "Saving, Investment and Growth in Eastern Europe," *IMF Working Paper* 91/61 (1991).

—— and J. Ostrey, "Structural and Macroeconomic Determinants of the Output Decline in Czechoslovakia and Poland," *IMF Working Paper* 92/86 (Washington, D.C.: International Monetary Fund, 1992).

——, Dimitri G. Demekas and Jonathan D. Ostry, "An Empirical Analysis of the Output Decline in Three Eastern European Countries," *IMF Staff Papers* V, 40 (1) (March 1993), 1–31.

Brada, Joseph C. and Arthur E. King, "Is There a J. Curve for the Economic Transition from Socialism to Capitalism?" In Kazimier Z. Poznanski, ed., *Stabilization and Privatization in Poland* (Norwell: Kluwer Academic Publishers, 1993), 251–269.

Brainard, William C. and James Tobin, "Pitfalls in Financial Model Building," *American Economic Review* 58 (1968), 99–122.

Bruno, Michael, "Stabilization and Reform in Eastern Europe: A Preliminary Evaluation," *IMF Staff Papers* 39 (4) (Dec. 1992), 19–49.

—— *Crisis, Stabilization and Economic Reform* (Oxford: Oxford University Press, 1993).

Buch, Claudia, "An Institutional Approach for Banking Reform in Eastern Europe," *Kiel Working Paper* 560 (1993).

Calvo, Guillermo A. and Manmohan S. Kumar, "Financial Markets and Intermediation (Part I). Financial Sector Reforms and Exchange Arrangements in Eastern Europe," *IMF Occasional Paper* 102 (1993).

—— "Financial Markets and Intermediation," in *Financial Sector Reforms and Exchange Arrangements in Eastern Europe*, *IMF Occasional Paper* 102 (1993).

—— "Money Demand, Bank Credit, and Economic Performance in Former Socialist Economies," *IMF Staff Papers* V, 41 (June 1994), 314–495.

Calvo, Guillermo A. and Jacob A. Frankel, "Credit Markets, Credibility, and Economic Transformation," *Journal of Economic Perspectives* 5 (4) (Fall 1991), 139–148.

Calvo, Guillermo and Fabrizio Coricelli, "Stagflationary Effects of Stabilization Programs in Reforming Socialist Countries: Enterprise-Side vs. Household-Side Factors," *The World Bank Economic Review* V, 6 (Jan. 1992).

—— "Output Collapse in Eastern Europe: The Role of Credit," *IMF Staff Papers* V, 40 (1) (March 1993), 32–52.

Calvo, Guillermo A., Manmohan S. Kumar, Eduardo Borensztein and Paul Masson, "Financial Sector Reforms and Exchange Arrangements in Eastern Europe," *IMF Occasional Paper* 102 (Feb. 1993).

Catte, Pietro and Christina Mastropasqua, "Financial Structure and Reforms in Central and Eastern Europe in the 1980s," *Journal of Banking and Finance* 17: 1 (1991), 57–75.

Central Statistical Office, *Statistical Bulletin* (Monthly), various issues.

Charemza, Wojciech W., "East European Transformation: The Supply Side," in

Kazimier Z. Poznanski, ed., *Stabilization and Privatization in Poland* (Norwell: Kluwer Academic Publishers, 1993), 151–171.

Claessens, S. and D. Naudé, *Recent Estimates of Capital Flight*, Policy Research Working Papers, WPS 1186 (Washington, D.C.: World Bank, 1993).

Clague, C. and G. Rausser, eds, *The Emergence of Market Economies in Eastern Europe* (Cambridge: Blackwell, 1992).

Corbett, Jenny and Colin Mayer, "Financial Reform in Eastern Europe: Progress with the Wrong Model," *Oxford Review of Economic Policy* V, 7:4 (1991), 57–75.

Courakis, A.S., "Modelling Portfolio Selection," *The Economic Journal* 98 (1988), 619–642.

Csaba, Laszlo, "Hungary and the IMF: The Experience of a Cordial Discord," *Journal of Comparative Economics* 20 (1995), 211–234.

Davis, Kemal and Timothy Cordon, "Hungary – Partial Successes and Remaining Challenges: The Emergence of a 'Gradualist' Success Story?" In Oliver Jean Blanchard, Kenneth A. Froot, and Jeffrey D. Sachs, eds, *The Transition in Eastern Europe*, vol. 1 (Chicago: University of Chicago Press, 1994), 123–153.

de Crombrugghe, Alain and David Lipton, "The Government Budget and the Economic Transformation of Poland," in Oliver Jean Blanchard, Kenneth A. Froot, and Jeffrey D. Sachs, *The Transition in Eastern Europe*, vol. 2 (Chicago: University of Chicago Press, 1994), 111–133.

Dittus, Peter, "Bank Reform and Behaviour in Central Europe," *Journal of Comparative Economics* 19 (3) (December 1994), 335–361.

Drabek, Zdenek, "IMF and IBRD Policies in the Former Czechoslovakia," *Journal of Comparative Economics* 20 (1995), 235–264.

Dyba, Karel and Jan Svejnar, "Stabilization and Transition in Czechoslovakia," in Oliver Jean Blanchard, Kenneth A. Froot, and Jeffrey D. Sachs, eds, *The Transition in Eastern Europe*, vol. 1 (Chicago: University of Chicago Press, 1994), 93–122.

Easterly, William and Paulo Vilira Da Cunha, "Financing the Storm: Macroeconomic Crisis in Russia," *Economic Transition* 2 (Dec. 1994), 443–466.

Ebrill, Liam P., Charalambos Ajai Chopra, Paul Mylonas, Inci Otker and Gerd Schwartz, "Poland: The Path to a Market Economy," *IMF Occasional Paper* 113 (Oct. 1994).

Edwards, Sebastian, "Stabilization and Liberalization Policies in Eastern Europe: Lessons from Latin America," in Christopher Clague and Gordon Rausser, eds, *The Emergence of Market Economies in Eastern Europe* (Oxford: Blackwell, 1992).

Ellman, Michael, "Transformation, Depression, and Economics: Some Lessons," *Journal of Comparative Economics* 19 (1) (August 1994), 1–21.

Estrin, Saul and Xavier Richet, "Industrial Adjustment and Restructuring in Poland: A Cross-Sectoral Approach," *Comparative Economic Studies* 35 (Winter 1993), 1–20.

European Bank for Reconstruction and Development, *Transition Report* (London: EBRD, 1995).

Farrell, John P., ed., "The Economic Transition in Eastern Europe," *Comparative Economic Studies* 33 (Summer 1991), 1–177.

Fischer, Stanley and Alan Gelb, "Issues in the Reform of Socialist Economies," in Vittitio Corbo *et al.*, eds, *Reforming Central and Eastern European Economies. Initial Results and Challenges* (Washington, D.C.: World Bank, 1991).

Funke, Norbert, "Timing and Sequencing of Reforms: Competing Views and the Role of Credibility," *Kyklos* 3 (1993), 337–362.

Gajdeczka, Przemyslaw T., "Inflation Tax, Household Wealth, and Privatization in Poland," in Kazimier Z. Poznanski, ed., *Stabilization and Privatization in Poland* (Norwell: Kluwer Academic Publishers, 1993), 173–195.

Gomulka, Stanislaw, "Polish Economic Reform 1990–1991: Principles, Policies, and Outcomes," *Cambridge Journal of Economics* 16 (Sept. 1992), 355–372.

—— "The Financial Situation of Enterprises and Its Impact on Monetary and Fiscal Policies: Poland 1992–93," *Economic Transition* 2 (June 1994a), 189–208.

—— "Budget Deficit and Inflation in Transition Economies," in V. Barta and C.M. Schneider, eds, *Stabilization Policies at Crossroads?* (Laxenburg: IIAS, 1994b).

—— "The IMF-Supported Programs of Poland and Russia, 1990–1994: Principles, Errors, and Results," *Journal of Comparative Economics* 20 (1995), 316–346.

Gowland, David H., *Finance in Eastern Europe* (Dartmouth: Aldershot, 1992).

Gupta, Kanhaya L. and Robert Lensink, *Financial Liberalization and Investment* (London: Routledge, 1996a).

—— "Rozwój Sektora Finansowego W Polsce: Prodejscie Symulcyjne I Wstepna Specyfikacja Modelu," in Alfred Janc and Tadeusz Kowalski, eds, *Reformy Finansowe W Krajach Tworzacych Gospodarke Rynkowa* (Poznan: Akademia Ekonomiczna W Poznaniu, 1996b), 51–81.

—— "Financial Reforms and Commercial Bank Behavior in Poland," in K.L. Gupta, ed., *Experiences with Financial Liberalization* (Boston: Kluwer Academic Publishers, 1997), 217–240.

Handler, H. and J. Stankovsky, *Financial Perspective of the Eastern Countries* (Vienna: WIFO, Nov. 1992).

Hare, P.G., "Hungary: In Transition to a Market Economy," *Journal of Economic Perspectives* 5, 4 (1991), 195–202.

Havlik, Peter, "Money Demand, Bank Credit, and Economic Performance in Former Socialist Economies," *IMF Working Paper* WP/94/3 (Jan. 1994).

Hermes, Niels and Robert Lensink, "The Magnitude and Determinants of Capital Flight: The Case for Six Sub-Saharan African Countries," *De Economist* 140 (1992), 515–530.

Hillman, A.L., "Macroeconomic Policy in Hungary and Its Microeconomic Implications," *European Economy* 43 (March 1990), 55–60.

Hogan, Daniel, Elizabeth Ryne and David Dad, *Poland's Emerging Financial System: Status and Prospects*, Report of the US Agency to International Development (Washington: USAID, Aug. 1993).

Hrncir, Miroslav, "Reforms of the Banking Sector in the Czech Republic," in John P. Bonin and P. Szekely Istsnan, eds, *The Development and Reform of Financial Systems in Central and Eastern Europe* (Aldershot: Edward Elgar, 1994), 221–256.

Kawalee, Stefan, Slawomir Sikosa, and Piotr Rymaszewski, "Dealing with Bad Debts: The Case of Poland," in Gerard Caprio *et al.*, eds, *Building Sound Finance in Emerging Market Economies* (Washington, D.C.: IMF and World Bank, 1994), 51–59.

Keating, G., "The Financial Sector of the London Business Scholl Model," in D. Currie, ed., *Advances in Monetary Economics* (London: Croom Helm, 1985), 86–126.

Korford, Kenneth J., ed., "Symposium: Economic Reform in Eastern Europe and the Former Soviet Union," *Eastern Economic Journal* 19 (Summer 1993), 329–393.

Kokoszcznski, Ryszard, "Money and Capital Market Reform in Poland," in John P. Bonin and Istnan P. Szeckely, eds, *The Development and Reform of Financial Systems in Central and Eastern Europe* (Aldershot: Edward Elgar, 1994), 257–267.

Kroonenberg, S., *Guess (Groningen University Econometric Simulation System: user's manual)* (Groningen: University of Groningen, 1991).

Kuipers, Simon K., Ben W.A. Jongbloed, Gerard H. Kuper and Elmer Sterken, *Het CCSO Jaarmodel van de Nederlandse Economie* (Groningen: Wolters-Noordhoff, 1988).

Layard, Richard, "Can Russia Control Inflation?" in J. Onno De Beaufort Wingnholds, *et al.*, eds, *A Framework for Monetary Stability* (New York: Kluwer Academic Publishers, 1994).

Leeds, Eva Marikova, "Voucher Privatization in Czechoslovakia," *Comparative Economic Studies* 35 (Fall 1993), 19–38.

Lensink, Robert, Niels Hermes and Victor Murinde, "Does Financial Liberalization Reduce Capital Flight?" *Discussion Papers in Corporate Finance* no. 03–96 (Birmingham: The University of Birmingham, Corporate Finance Research, 1996).

Lipton, David and Jeffrey Sachs, "Privatization in Eastern Europe: The Case of Poland," *Brookings Papers on Economic Activity* 2 (1990), 293–341.

Long, M. and S. Sagari, "Financial Reform in Socialist Economies in Transition," *World Bank PRD Working Paper* 70.711 (1991).

Mayer, C. and X. Vines, *Capital Markets and Financial Intermediation* (Cambridge: Cambridge University Press, 1993).

Murinde, Victor, Niels Hermes and Robert Lensink, "Comparative Aspects of the Magnitude and Determinants of Capital Flight in Six-Subsaharan African Countries," *Savings and Development* (1996), 61–78.

Narodowy Bank Polski (NBP), *Information Bulletin*, various issues.

Nijsse, E. and E. Sterken, "Shortages, Interest Rates, and Money Demand in Poland, 1969–1994," Unpublished paper, Department of Economics, University of Groningen (July 1995).

Nuti, D.M., "Internal and International Aspects of Monetary Disequilibrium in Poland," *European Economy* 43 (March 1990), 169–182.

Nyers, Reszo and Gabrilla Lutz, "The Structural Reform of the Banking System in Hungary: The Solution of the Problem of Bad Debts in the Hungarian Banking System," *OECD Document CCEET/DAFFE/CMF/RD* (92) 38 (1992).

O'Brien, R., ed., *Finance in the International Economy* (Oxford: Oxford University Press, 1992).

Organization for Economic Cooperation and Development, *OECD Economic Surveys: Czech and Slovak Federal Republic* (Paris: OECD, 1991).

—— *Economic Survey of Poland* (Paris: OECD, 1992).

—— *Economic Survey of Hungary* (Paris: OECD, 1993).

—— *Economic Survey of the Czech and Slovak Republics* (Paris: OECD, 1994).

Owen, P.D., "Dynamic Models of Portfolio Behavior: A General Integrated Model of Incorporating Sequential Effects," *American Economic Review* 71 (1981), 231–238.

Parkin, Michael J. "Discount House Portfolio and Debt Selection," *Review of Economic Studies* 37 (1970), 469–497.

——, R.J. Cooper, F.J. Henderson and M.K. Danes, "An Integrated Model of Consumption, Investment and Portfolio Decisions," Reserve Bank of Australia, *Papers in Monetary Economics* vol. II (1975).

PlanEcon Report, various issues.

Polanski, Zbigniew, "The Polish Experience: The Financial System, Economic Development, and Macroeconomic Policies in Post-Communist Countries," in D.H. Gowland, ed., *Finance in Eastern Europe* (Dartmouth: Aldershot, 1992).

—— "Credit and Monetary Policy and the Financial System in Poland, 1990–93," *Russian and East European Finance and Trade* (Sept./Oct. 1994), 53–84.

Portes, Richard, "Transformation Traps," *Economic Journal* 106 (Sept. 1994), 1178–1189.

Poznanski, Kazimierz Z., *Stabilization and Privatization in Poland: An Economic Evaluation of the Shock Therapy Program* (Boston: Kluwer Academic Publishers, 1993).

Purvis, Douglas C., "Dynamic Models of Portfolio Behavior: More Pitfalls in Financial Model Building," *American Economic Review* 68 (1978), 147–168.

Riecke, Werner, "Managing Foreign Debt and Monetary Policy During Transformation," in P. Istnar Szekely and David M.G. Newberry, eds, *Hungary – An Economy in Transition* (Cambridge/New York: Cambridge University Press and CEPR, 1994), 224–230.

Rodlauer, Markus, "The Experience with IMF-Supported Reform Programs in Central and Eastern Europe," *Journal of Comparative Economics* 20 (1995), 95–115.

Roley, Vance V., "Symmetry Restrictions in a System of Financial Asset Demands: Theoretical and Empirical Results," *Review of Economics and Statistics*, LXV, 1983, 124–130.

Sachs, Jeffrey, "The Economic Transformation of Eastern Europe," in Kazimier Z. Poznanski, ed., *Stabilization and Privatization in Poland* (Norwell: Kluwer Academic Publishers, 1993), 197–212.

Santomero, A.M., "Modeling the Banking Firm: A Survey," *Journal of Money, Credit, and Banking* 16 (1984), 576–602.

Shew, Raphael, *Economic Reform in Poland and Czechoslovakia* (Westport, CT: Praeger, 1993).

Siklos, Peter L. and Iran Abel, "The Credit Crunch as a Disinflation Strategy: Exchange Rate and Monetary Policy in the Transition to Market in Hungary, Poland and Czechoslovakia," in Richard D. Sweeney, Claes Wihlborg and Thomas D. Willett, eds, *Establishing Monetary Stability in Emerging Market Economies* (Boulder, CO: Westview Press, 1993).

Smith, G., "Dynamic Models of Portfolio Behavior: Comment on Purvis," *American Economic Review* 68 (1978), 410–416.

Sterken, Elmer, "Integrated Real-Financial Modelling: A Macro Econometric Application for the Dutch Economy," *Economic Modelling* 8 (1991), 130–174.

Sundrarajan, V., "Financial Sector Reform and Central Banking in Centrally Planned Economies," *IMF Central Banking Department Working Paper* 90/120 (1990).

Swank, Job, *Bank Behaviour and Monetary Policy in the Netherlands: Theory and Evidence*, PhD Thesis, Free University of Amsterdam, 1994.

Szekely, I., "The Reform of the Hungarian Financial System," *European Economy* 43 (March 1990), 107–124.

Thakor, Anjan, "The Design of Financial Systems: an Overview," *Journal of Banking and Finance* 20 (1996), 917–948.

Thorne, A., "Eastern Europe's Experience with Banking Reform: Is There a Role for Banks in the Transition?" *Journal of Banking and Finance* 17 (1993), 959–1000.

van Brabant, Jozef M., "Lessons from the Wholesale Transformation in the East," *Journal of Comparative Economics* 35 (Winter 1993a), 73–102.

—— , ed., *The New Eastern Europe and the World Economy* (Boulder, CO: Westview, 1993a).

van Erp, F.A.M., B.H. Hasselman, A.G.H. Nibbelink and H.R. Timmer, "A Monetary Model of the Dutch Economy: A Quarterly Submodel of FREIA-Kompas," *Economic Modelling* 6 (1989), 59–93.

van Wijnbergen, Sweder, "On the Role of Banks in Enterprise Restructuring: The Polish Example," *CEPR Discussion Paper* No. 898 (December 1993).

—— , "Eastern Europe After the First Five Years," Mimeo (July 1994).

Varhegy, Eva, "The Second Reform of the Hungarian Banking System," in John P. Bonin and Istran P. Szeckely, eds, *The Development and Reform of Financial Systems in Central and Eastern Europe* (Aldershot: Edward Elgar, 1994), 293–308.

Vojtisek, Petr, "Strategies for Solving the Bad Debt Problems of Banks – Overview of Main Issues: The Czechoslovakia Case," paper presented at OECD DAFFE meeting in Paris (1992).

Wallich, Christine I., "What's Right and Wrong With World Bank Involvement in Eastern Europe," *Journal of Comparative Economics* 20 (1995), 57–94.

Winiecki, Jan, "The Applicability of Standard Reform Packages to Eastern Europe," *Journal of Comparative Economics* 20 (1995), 347–367.

Wyczanski, Pawel, "The Polish Banking System, 1990–92," Friedrich Ebert Foundation, Economic and Social Policy Series, no. 32 (Warsaw, 1993).

Zecchini, Salvatore, "The Role of International Financial Institutions in the Transition Process," *Journal of Comparative Economics* 20 (1995), 116–138.

INDEX

adding-up restrictions 27, 48–9
adjustment costs 23–4, 24
asset demand equations: commercial
   banks 22–7, 88–9; firms 73–4, 91–2;
   households 45–9, 90

bad loans 15, 30–1
balance of payments 99
Baltensberger, E. 22
bank loans: to firms 132–3 (comparison
   of transitional economies 15–17;
   effects of changes in discount rate on
   supply 109–10; effects of changes in
   required reserve ratios 114–16; effects
   of loan and default rate changes on
   supply 118–20, 127; increase in
   supply 83–4; and investment 68–70,
   76; model for firms 73–4, 76; nominal
   stock 152–3; portfolio composition
   for commercial banks 18–21, 34; rates
   of return 20–1, 27–8, 29–32, 37–40,
   142–3); to households 18–21;
   'non-performing' loans 15, 30–1; *see
   also* central bank loans, lending rates
banking sector 14–17; *see also* central
   bank, commercial banks
Berg, A. 14
'big bang' approach 1
Blanchard, O.J. 13, 14
bonds, long-term 18, 28, 93–4; *see also*
   government securities
Borensztein, E. 13–14
Brainard, W.C. 22, 25, 46
broad money/GDP ratio 14–15
budget constraints 103; central bank 96;
   commercial banks 88; firms 73, 91;
   government 98; households 44–5,
   89–90

budget deficits 94, 98
budget law 94
Bulgaria 13–14

Calvo, G.A. 14, 100
capital flight 50
capital flows 99
capital stock: dynamic simulation with
   complete model 103–7; effects of
   changes in discount rate 110–12;
   effects of loan and default rate
   changes 119–20, 121; effects of zloty
   time deposit rate changes 122, 124;
   model for firms 73–4, 78, 79, 82;
   nominal 152–3
central bank (NBP) 5, 92–8, 104; effects
   of changes in the discount rate 6,
   108–12; effects of changes in required
   reserve ratios 6, 113–16, 126–7;
   nominal foreign reserves 162–3
central bank loans: to commercial
   banks 18–21, 34, 35, 92–3, 132–3
   (effects of changes in discount rate
   110, 111; impact of increased
   lending rate on share 37–40;
   lending rate 28, 108–12, 142–3); to
   government 92–4, 98
central government *see* government
choice-theoretic approach to asset
   demand functions 22–5
Claessens, S. 50
coefficient of determination: commercial
   banks 33–4, 35; firms 82; households
   51–6
commercial banks 3–4, 18–40; central
   bank lending to *see* central bank loans;
   effects of changes in discount rate
   108–12; effects of changes in required

187